ISBN: 978-1-946647-02-3

Printed in the United States of America

Published by Coyote Creek Books
www.coyotecreekbooks.com

Cover and illustrations by Cliff Helm.
www.Mayhem-Mediums.artistwebsites.com

MAYHEM

A LIFE

MAYHEM

A LIFE

Cliff Helm

Coyote Creek Books | San José | California

I would like to dedicate this book to my parents and family for standing by me and never giving up on me no matter how low or high my life fell or soared. They were always there for me. Thank you.

Table of Contents

Chapter 1: To Heaven and Back

I sat on the porch of the trailer at the base of the Sierra Mountains, right next door to Death Valley, waiting for the sun to set in the intense August heat. Little did I know how prophetic the words "Death Valley" would become. I was here to work on a drilling rig run by the father of one of my best friends. The job was in China Lake close to the Naval Weapons Station.

I had arrived earlier in the week to this stinking little trailer park, out in the middle of nowhere. The trailer park was typical, a collection of seedy run-down single-wide trailers one is used to seeing out in the middle of nowhere. One was to be my home for the time I was working. With its plain dirt yards and fifties-style trailers, it was no garden community.

The park included a tiny worn-down store that stocked the usual drinks and sundries.

About the only nice thing I can say about the place is that there was a swimming pool, water-stained and cracked as it may have been, an oasis out there in the middle of the desert. Sitting in that crappy little hellhole that day, I had no idea how close to death I was.

Nepotism aside, I suspect I got the job because of my size and strength. At 18 years old, I was an exceptionally big boy and an undefeated wrestler in high school for several years until I lost my knee in a match.

Prior to the knee injury, in the eighth grade I was wrestling 165 pounds, 185 pounds as sophomore, and in my junior year I wrestled 212 pounds. By my junior year I was able to power clean 315 pounds to my chest. I weighed in at 245 pounds in my senior year. This was mostly due to my upbringing on a ranch and bucking hay for my father all summer long. He was a hay contractor. He swathed and bailed the hay then paid my friends and me to buck it out of the field with hay hooks in hand. These bails can weigh anywhere from 145 to 245 pounds each, and when you have 3,2000 of them to get out of a field in forty-eight hours, you manage to get in shape.

I had always thought I would become a union structural ironworker like my dad. Tough job but decent pay. I never cared for school, and for this career a high school diploma wasn't needed, just a GED. My father had already helped a few of my friends into the union and they were all making over fifty grand a year at age nineteen and twenty. I had told my father when I was sixteen years old that I didn't want to go to school any longer, that I would rather join the union and make some money.

My father, being wise and knowing how stubborn I could be, told me if I could get my GED he would get me into the union. He didn't think I'd pass. To take the GED, you had to be seventeen. I lied. My size probably bolstered my deceitful claim.

I passed and had great expectations of moving immediately into a job, independence and adulthood.

My father, however, had other ideas. He listed my sports accomplishments: nearly undefeated for four years as a wrestler and the

Nevada state leader in tackles as a nose guard my junior year.

"You should at least stay in school and finish your senior year playing sports," he said.

"Who knows, I'm sure you can get a scholarship."

I had thought about it; in fact, I had often thought about going to school for art or graphic design. I had been painting with oils and acrylics since age eleven. My aunt and cousins, who were very good artists, had given me my first set of paints and brushes. During high school I created paintings from album covers, such as Grateful Dead's *Blues for Allah* and Pink Floyd's green pyramids from *Dark Side of the Moon*. I sold many of my paintings to my friends and family throughout out the years. At age fifteen, I was creating airbrush portraits.

While I didn't remain in school my whole senior year, I stayed until the end of football season.

I was expecting to go to work right away in the union. But life had a different plan. I had to find other work like delivering drilling mud to the various drilling sites around California, Nevada and Oregon until a big enough job came to Reno that would pull me into the ironworker's union for help. While I was doing my delivery job for Nova mud my old friend offered me the job on the drilling rig working for his father out near Death Valley. Danny was an old cowboy friend who used to high school rodeo with my sister Lucy, and they dated for a time. He and I became best friends, and our families did too. Short and strong, Danny had the looks along with the love of the *drink* of his Irish father and pulled the dark hair and dark eyes from his Mexican mother. Unlike his mother, he couldn't speak a lick of Spanish.

While I waited for the first day of my new job on the drilling rig, I found quite a few little streams around. Fishing made a good way to pass the time. I caught some of the abundant and brightly colored rainbow trout and German Browns. I hiked, searching for scenery. The area of the Sierras by Convict Lake is boundless and beautiful.

Finally, Danny arrived. We left the seedy trailer park and moved to a dumpy hotel. The view was dominated by tumbleweeds and Joshua trees. Because I had to be up by 4:30 a.m., I hit the sagging bed early, laying my head down on a rock hard, dusty pillow. The drilling site was a two-hour drive away.

I was new, so I was a rough neck. Even though it's a job on the bottom of the ladder, a roughneck is an important position that requires a great deal of stamina. A roughneck works alongside the pump man and the derrick man and everyone reports to the driller. My driller's name was Hambone.

It was hot, 118-degrees-in-the-shade kind of hot. With the big diesel engines continuously roaring, the clanking of the metal and spools, and the *clang clang* of the drilling, I could hardly think. Yelling was the only way to communicate.

My job was to remove the core drill pipe and empty the drill core out for the geologist, who tests the core samples. Core samples help determine if we are searching in the right areas.

The cable consistently winds around the spool as the pipe is pulled out of the ground. When the pipe is sent back down into the hole, the cable has to come off the spool to lower the pipe. When the pipe is pulled back out of the ground it wraps back on the spool. Sometimes this cable can gather at one end of the spool instead of spreading evenly like a spool of thread. When this happens, it needs to be pulled from the spool and then guided back on.

A cable is made up of many individual wires and then bundled for strength. Some wires develop spurs. If you happen to grab a spur it can cut you. If it grabs your glove you are in big trouble. Earlier that day, Hambone noticed the cable clumped up on one side of the spool. He told me to pull it off the spool and to hold the cable in my hand, guiding it evenly back onto the spool. Even though it went well, I imagined my hand getting caught up on a spur. Or being sucked into the cable. I didn't like this part of the job. It was very unnerving.

As the end of the workday neared, I was looking forward to quitting time. I looked up at my watch; in fifteen minutes, I'd be on my way to relaxing with a beer or two and a nice barbecued steak. I had brought a little Hibachi just for this occasion.

I was pondering that steak and cold beer when the cable wrapped up crookedly on the spool again. A bad feeling flushed under my skin when Hambone yelled for me to undo the cable and guide it back again.

As I started to pull the cable off the spool, I felt it sliding over my shoulder and down my back like a heavy snake. I kept pulling and pulling in attempt to unwrap it off the spool. Out of the corner of my eye, I saw that the cable had coiled over a rod that was connected to the rig on the far side of the spool. I thought if this cable engages into gear it will suck me right into the spool and I'm a goner.

At that very moment I heard a massive bang. It was as though the machine came alive, a vicious and powerful animal snapping its jaw shut. It grabbed my glove and started pulling me into its coils. I tried like hell to pull my hand out, but the cable had already sunk into my hand. I screamed, fearing for my life.

The cable buried itself into my left hand, crushing its way through. Mercilessly it smashed through my flesh and bones. I heard the bones being crushed like a roll of caps sounding off, like bubble wrap being popped.

The cable continued to claim my hand, a wrestling match from hell. Pulling with all my might did nothing. I was at the mercy of this hideous creature. It cut into my triceps, then dislocated my left shoulder and started to wrap me onto the spool across my back. As the cable tightened over my back, lifting me off the ground and coiling around me like a python crushing its prey, a warm numbing feeling began to engulf me. I could no longer breathe or move.

Suddenly I was seeing a day when I was four years old, crying because I'm bleeding; I've just run my wrists through a glass door. My mother holds ice on my wrists, cold and numbing, as we rush to the hospital. And I'm age six and can smell the fresh manure, dust and hay while standing in the dirt at the old corrals down on Pyramid Way with my grandfather when he purchased Tonka, my first black pony. I'm so excited to have my own horse. Then age seven: there sits in the living room on the red carpet my birthday present: a gold Stingray bicycle with banana seat.

One after another, important memories flew through me at lightning speed yet I saw every detail vividly as though time had taken on a new shape. I was flooded with an overwhelming feeling of peace, a sense of relief. An orgasmic ecstasy filled my soul. All worry pain and fear were sucked out of me. I was engulfed in a soothing peace, serenity like nothing I'd ever felt before.

Then it went dark. I was flying through some kind of tunnel. Ahead streamed a bright and soothing light. Not just a white light, more like a spectrum. I could see the bright yellows and the cool blues, I could feel the warmth of the reds. I knew that what lay ahead was so much better than what I was leaving. I had no concern for leaving my life or the people that were in it. In a split second all became clear: this life is the hell we have to pass through to get to heaven.

Suddenly I was back on the rig. Everyone was trying desperately to start the motor to put it in reverse. It was like a scene in a horror movie: the actor is trying to get away, while the lurking monster approaches and the car that won't start. The motor turned over and over. Still it wouldn't start. The men tried to pry the cable off of me with six-foot crowbars. Finally, the snake's coils loosened and I fell to my knees.

My left arm was dislocated where the cable had ripped it out of its socket. My thumb was flattened and left hanging by a sliver of flesh. I felt nothing.

Two men tossed me into the cab of a truck, flying sideways down the dirt road as we hauled ass towards a hospital. We passed Danny and his dad, who were on their way to relieve the day crew.

After an hour or so I was starting to hurt. Pain wracked my body with such intensity that I thrashed about, tearing up the insides of the truck. I tore the dash off and the headliner out. I was kicking the dash in where the ashtray and glove box were once located. All I could think of was the pain. Over and over I hit my head against the window.

When we got to Big Pine, the medics said to keep going; they had no resources to treat the severity of my injuries. We flew down the highway at ninety miles an hour towards the next town, Lone Pine, only to be told the same thing.

With no relief for the pain I sank into shock. My whole body was throbbing in sync with the beat of my heart. Pain absorbed me and entered every cell, every thought.

Heaven had disappeared as surely as hell had returned.

Chapter 2: One Hundred and Eighty Degrees

It had been two or three years since my accident in Death Valley on the drilling rig. Since then, I'd undergone four surgeries with Dr. McCuskey. An orthopedic surgeon, Dr. McCuskey had previously performed a few knee surgeries on me during wrestling season when I was in high school.

He'd sewed my thumb back on, but it was black and had no feeling. With each surgery, it seemed like he took a hatchet and chopped off a little more to get to where the blood was circulating. Now with my thumb almost gone and full of pins and metal, my hand creeped me out. It looked like a foreign creature. And it hurt. Even though I had not much thumb and no nail, it felt like someone was pressing down on the nail. Phantom limb, I was told. This painful sensation would last for five years.

After I completed the thumb surgeries, I was looking at vocational rehabilitation. I was twenty years old and trying to think of what I'd like to do the rest of my life. My uncle Ed, who was married to my mother's sister Georgia and was a consultant for IBM in Illinois, told my mother if I wanted to learn computers, he would teach me. Computers? The only ones I'd seen were Apple computers in my high school in the early eighties. I could not for the life of me figure out why anyone would want to learn that stuff.

At that time, I was living with my sister Kathy and her new boyfriend, Grant.

My free time was winding down. Finally, I was going to be able to pick a career and or start some kind of schooling or trade. I'd been enjoying my time off. I made a few trips down to see my cousin Mike in L.A. He was the lucky one with a fast metabolism. Somehow Mike could eat and drink anything and always retain that tortoise shell stomach and six pack abs. Growing up mainly on Santa Monica Beach, Pier 17, he was always that *Bain De Soleil*, golden brown color. The blond hair blue eyed Romeo always sported a hot girl, and from a country boy's point of view, he lived every red-blooded American boy's dream of growing up on the beach surfing and chasing bikinis all day. I always looked forward to trips down then dreaded the trips coming back to Reno. I didn't want to leave the nice warm climate, the beautiful women who seemed so much easier to talk to and easier to pick up on than the stuck-up girls in the Reno area. The women of Reno had nothing on these sun drenched golden beauties of Southern California, yet for some reason they all seemed to have some kind of attitude, like their shit didn't stink. The southern beauties not only out-looked them but also out-classed them and usually had much more going for themselves, like money and an education along with looks that killed. Maybe the Reno attitude had to do with the woman shortage. They knew the laws of shortage in demand.

Kathy's best friend Liza was always around. I'd had a crush on her since I was sixteen. She always had a smile and a joke, kind of a bust-your-chops sense of humor. She was older than Kathy, yet seemed younger at heart. Portuguese with dishwater blond hair and piercing hazel eyes, she filled out her jeans in all the right spots. Even though I was much younger, she would always flirt around with me.

One night I awoke with Liza's tan, smooth, sexy body lying next to me. She and Kathy must have gotten home late after a night on the town. Giggling, rubbing up against me and kissing me, she asked, "Do you mind if I stay?" Kissing her back I let her know I would not mind at all. Finally, at age twenty, my teenage dream was coming true.

Soon Liza and I were spending a lot of time together. One day as were enjoying a great day up at Lake Tahoe on the beach, she said, "Have you ever thought about becoming a hairdresser? Maybe you should go to beauty college."

I looked at her out the corner of my eye. "No fucking way! Are you crazy?" Liza worked as a barber, but I thought only gay guys went to beauty college.

"You need a career. It's steady, and you can make a lot of money."

"Liza," I said. "I'm not gay. That just won't work for me."

"Trust me," she said. "You'll make big bucks. And it's creative and fun."

"Listen, Liza," I said. "I played hard football and was an undefeated wrestler. I rode bulls and bareback broncs in the rodeo. A hairdresser? Right. And what would my father and friends think?"

Liza laughed. Then she told me about the movie *Shampoo*, where Warren Beatty gets a lot of pussy as a hairdresser.

A few nights later, my friends and I went out to a nightclub. We approached a few girls, and we were talking smack as usual.

"What do you guys do?" asked a little blond hottie in a short black skirt.

My friends started chiming in: *I'm an ironworker, I'm a carpenter,*

I'm a concrete finisher.

Then all eyes turn to me, wanting to see the girls' reaction.

"I'm thinking about going to beauty college," I said.

The girls gathered around me, grabbing my arms and shoulders and asking what I would do with their hair.

Warren Beatty, indeed. My face lit up with a shit-eating grin. At that moment I knew yes, I wanted to do hair.

When I first enrolled in cosmetology courses, I was nervous. I was doing a one hundred and eighty-degree career change: roughneck to softneck. My first day of class I was happy to see Jane Mayhill, a bubbly brunette who'd gone to my high school in Fallon. Her face was lit up with her trademark wide smile. I had grown up knowing her and her family through high school rodeos. I had ridden a little rough stock, bulls and bareback broncs. My sister use to run poles and barrels and breakaway roping. It was a very close-knit community.

Then I noticed another friend from Fallon, Chuck, who'd hurt his back at work and was changing professions, too. He always had a great sense of humor. Never a bad day that guy. And what a relief, I wasn't the only straight guy.

Our first lesson was shampoo sets. If you became good at these all the old ladies or "Blue Hairs" as we called them would request you. Then you would be doing shampoo sets all day. I tried to avoid these shampoo sets by shaving racing stripes on one side of my mannequin's head and a checkerboard pattern on the other side, topped off with a mohawk, dying her orange and blond, and mounting her right up front on my station. I would hear the old ladies getting blue hair and shampoo sets say, "Oh my God, look at what he did to that poor doll's hair. I would never let him touch my hair!"

I laughed. Just what I was trying to achieve.

I can still remember standing there watching the instructor evaluate my first few haircuts. I couldn't wait for the day that I'd know how to cut the whole head of hair from beginning to end.

I got very nervous when the first few people sat in my chair for a cut. Especially the first time. It looked so easy. Yet when it came for the second and third snip? I couldn't remember what to do. Standing there sweating and turning red, I squealed to the instructor for help. But I stumbled through, learning my way and my style. The key was to stay busy and get all the experience I could before going out on the street.

The owner of the school had a son named Dale, who had exceptional mannerisms, a very refined style and a great dress code. He always looked prim and proper not a hair misplaced. He usually wore slacks with stylish shirts and nice shoes. If Bob Ross, the TV show artist, had an equal for hair it was Dale: brown hair worn in a tight curl perm- almost afro that he kept finely manicured, always teasing at it with his pick. He was not a very big guy and had a feminine frame. Like me, he liked things very neat and organized. He had a positive attitude, and very good sense of humor.

One night, a group of us from school were out having a few drinks at a club and the girls were trying to get Dale to dance with them. I have no rhythm so avoided dancing like the plague. Dale had no problem dancing, but when one of the girls tried to kiss him, he turned away, a look of disgust burning in his eyes. Kind of like the look I would have if a guy tried to kiss me. That's when it clicked; he was gay. I had an idea he was, but now I knew it to be true. It took me a while to accept it. Eventually, it did not matter whether he was gay or not. He became one of my first best gay friends of many in that field.

Dale and I often disappeared upstairs to the facial room to smoke a joint. Later, Dale would just sit back and put me up at the register; he knew I was great at pushing products. He taught me to be good at what I did. He would always preach, "Consult, suggest and then recommend." That formula worked well. So after listening to what my client wanted, I would make recommendations, which would include some kind of chemical service like a color or perm (or maybe both), along with a facial and nails. We would see how many services we could do on one client rather than how many clients we could do one service on.

One day, as Dale was helping me study for boards, as we were sitting in the back of the class he said, "Cliff, so tell me how many of these girls have been with?"

There were twenty-three girls in the class.

"Nineteen."

We looked at each other and he started laughing. Yes, I learned to love beauty college and the profession.

I would often get requests for *the guy with one thumb*. It was strange at first, but then I got used to it. I was not offended. At least they remembered me. Because of my thumb, it was difficult not to drop the comb and I had to come up with my own way to wrap perms. Most people didn't even notice. But when someone would ask me how I became a hairdresser I would show them my thumb and tell them about the accident on the drilling rig. When they could not remember my name, they could remember I had only one thumb.

After working for a while in Reno, I started to get bored. I started thinking I would like to learn more about the latest fashions and designs, maybe even get somewhere I could be doing the hair of rock stars or movie stars. I knew I had to get back down to Southern California to do this. I got hired at Salon Valentino's, in San Clemente, California working for Adrian, a very polite man in his fifties with dark eyes framed by tortoise shell glasses. He had dark brown hair with a little gray that he wore straight with a little sweep to the left on top. He was very busy, in high demand, making eighteen hundred dollars a day. With the help of his shampoo boy, Greg, Adrian was always working on at least three clients at a time. Greg was a riot. His looks matched his personality, tall with a belly and curly wild eighties hairstyle. It didn't take me long to figure out they were a couple. I'd come a long way from my small town, conservative life.

I loved that job. We were practically on the beach. On a good day we would put the clients to process out on the back patio with the view of Catalina Island. Featuring bold reds and golds, the salon had a vibrant upbeat feel. We whipped up margaritas to please our clients.

There were eight stations Adrian was renting out at a time for eight hundred a month each. It was all women, including Adrian's daughter Christina. She was gorgeous and blond with beautiful brown eyes. Her attitude made it clear she knew she was all that plus some.

The stylists became my family, the salon my home away from home. We did fun things together, like go to the movies and out to nightclubs. On our way to see *Little Shop of Horrors,* four of us sat in the car, secretly smoking a joint before we got there so Adrian wouldn't know. Greg, who deliberately sat next to me in the back seat, gave me his Cheshire cat smile as he handed me the joint.

"You're going to want me one day, you know."

I laughed as I took the joint.

"Sorry, buddy, isn't going to happen," I said. I was uncomfortable, but he was my friend. It was kind of fun that we could joke about this. He knew not to push too far. I thought if my friends back in Reno saw me now, they'd be shocked.

"You never know," he said looking mischievously out the corner of his eye.

"You know who I could see myself with?" I said. "Christina. Adrian's daughter. She's smokin' hot.

"Whatever," he said, rolling his eyes.

One day, a gorgeous woman walked into the salon. Her stunning smile was just as impressive as her body. Her name was Katrina. She had a fun accent that I liked and was drawn to. As I did her shampoo, I asked her where she was from. She told me she was from Canada visiting her father for a week or so. She worked as a flight attendant.

We met down at the pier later that night for dinner and drinks. Then we decided to go to the natural hot springs on the Ortega highway for a soak. Neither of us had a bathing suit but we did have a buzz, so who cared? We had an exciting time finding our sensual chemistry together.

The next day she invited me to have dinner at her father's home; the invitation was actually his idea. During this meal I learned that Katrina had recently lost her brother in a motorcycle accident. In the pictures I noticed he looked a lot like me. Dark wavy brown hair and blue eyes. Later that evening, her father said I was welcome to spend the night.

"My father must really like you, Cliff. He's never allowed a man to stay the night with me much less invited one," Katrina said. "I think you remind him of Alex." She teared up, and I pulled her into my arms.

Katrina's father was a multimillionaire who owned a company that made custom wood handrails out of Canada. One day he told us, if we married, he would purchase us a home anywhere we wanted. A dream come true. We opened joint accounts together, working to build something so we could get her a green card. We had talked about how we wanted a house by the beach in Carlsbad. Her family owned a condo there. We'd often go and play house, imagining we were living there together. We loved the smell and feel of the salt air. I could picture us together in a very happy life.

Eventually, I changed salons, moving to South Coast Plaza in Costa Mesa, one of the largest malls in the nation. I was stoked. There were so many clients. Not just any clients: beautiful women everywhere I looked.

Some with long sleek ponytails, others with flowing curls. Hotties with curvy bodies, cuties with tiny fingers and turned up noses. As the days passed and I feasted my eyes on this girl buffet, I thought, *how could I marry one woman?*

I had to tell Katrina I could not plan to be with her any longer. I didn't want to lead her on or hurt her. I did not understand the gravity of this loss until much later. Losing good things became a bad habit of mine.

It was fascinating to do hair in Southern California. Some days I would have a beautiful woman in my chair explaining to me in a heavy accent about her country. Many people coming from other countries liked to go to salons in New York or Los Angeles where they could get the latest fashionable cut. What international enrichment for this small town boy.

One incident that was truly prophetic came to light as I was doing hair at Golden Shears. An elderly woman who was an attorney started to come and see me.

One day I was working on her hair, like all good stylists, I'd started to build a professional relationship with her.

"So why did you come to me?" I asked.

"The woman I went to for years did a great job but unfortunately she had a horrible accident. She had put her right hand through a glass window, cutting all the muscles and tendons from wrist to elbow. She will probably lose her right hand."

I would be devastated if something like that happened to me, I thought. Although I'd come awfully close to such a scenario in the drilling rig accident, fortunately I could work with one thumb. I loved doing hair, living the life like Warren Beatty in *Shampoo*. I loved the company of women, flirting with them, making them happy. My work was play. I couldn't envision doing anything else.

A few months later, my sister called, telling me that my parents were having relationship difficulties. She said I should come back to

Reno and be there for the family. I never thought my parents' relationship would be in peril. On Oct. 30, 1987, I packed my stuff and threw all I owned in the back of my 1959 Ford truck.

As I drove into the mountains, the air cooled. I needed to change from my shorts and tank top into pants and a sweatshirt. At six thousand feet elevation I had to put on my down jacket. What the hell was I doing? Why was I going back when I had it made down in Southern California?

But as destiny would have it I would end up back in Reno.

Chapter 3: The Final Trip

My sister set me up with a job interview at De Cuts, a fairly new and promising salon. I knew I had made a mistake of a life time, when I asked my first client, "Where are you from?"

"Sun Valley," he said, referring to a little backwater town north of Reno. A place filled with druggies and couch potatoes.

My heart sank. I had regressed. Here I was, back in Reno, home of stagnation, no fashion and uninteresting people from nowhere. Most my clients would now be construction workers, casino workers or people from the local malls and fast food restaurants.

And I was barely making a cut a day because of such a small population. My parents soon worked their differences out after I got back home. I probably could have stayed in Southern California and they would have come to the same resolution.

I needed to supplement my income somehow.

I turned to my old friend Dave and his father, Big Ed.

Known as the Mill Street Gorilla, Big Ed owned a used car lot and often sold wholesale to the local car lots. Dave and I had been good friends for a few years. He had straight brown hair he wore in a mullet down past his collar and a Fu Machu mustache. At six foot six, he was very long and lean; his legs went clear up to my chest. An avid hunter and guide, he could walk very fast and leave the rest of the crew in the dust. I got a job helping him and his dad pick up and deliver cars.

On our trips to Roseville Toyota, Big Dave easily put away a case of beer while driving a one-ton Chevy ramp truck with one hand at up to one hundred miles per hour. And that was just on the way there. Sometimes we took this trip three times a day. Although I didn't drink beer, I'd smoke my share of weed.

After delivering cars, we'd end up at a local restaurant that had a bar and tiny dance hall. The place was quaint and had good food but we were more interested in the booze.

One night we were enjoying our drinks and bullshitting when out of nowhere a beer bottle crashed onto our table. We promptly jumped up. The next thing we knew we were in a fistfight. It was your typical bar fight. A bunch of drunken idiots wallowing around. I guess one of the idiots had thought we were evil eyeing them, when actually Dave, who probably needed glasses, had been squinting at the TV.

Dave and I were thrown out of the bar, so we jumped into an old wood side-paneled Plymouth station wagon. We didn't always get the best cars to drive. And when Big Ed was upset at Dave he would make him drive real shit boxes. Things like an old 68 station wagon or a yellow truck that looked like an old county truck beat to hell.

As we left the parking lot I noticed my right hand was swollen. I couldn't move my fingers. Dave took me to the hospital. After an eight-hour tour through ER, I left with a cast on my right hand.

The next weekend I was sent to Modesto to pick up a Jeep Eagle 4-wheel drive car for Big Ed. I got back to Reno about 11 p.m. on a Saturday Night. Reno doesn't even start to wake up until midnight. I had a cast on my right hand, yet this wouldn't hinder my next adventure.

It was the night before Mother's Day. I planned to go to my parents' ranch in Fallon the next day for a celebration with my mom. In the meantime, I wanted to find some excitement. I was wide-awake in that way you get after driving a long time. Over stimulated, I headed to a local rocker bar, Del Mar Station. I was there just an hour when I made eye contact with a very cute brunette wearing a sexy little mini skirt and fishnet stockings. Over drinks, we yelled at the top of our lungs above the music. I asked her if she would like to go back to my place. She thought that was a great idea. Soon we were heading south on Virginia Street and making out at the stoplights.

Just a few weeks before, I had seen a movie where a couple had sex while driving down the road in a '56 Ford pickup. *Wow what could be better than that?* I had thought. And now it was happening! She climbed on top of me.

What the movie didn't show was the windshield fogging up. Suddenly my vision was blurred. I then turned down Grove Street and hit the defroster on high. We were still at it; it was incredible! But I couldn't see a damn thing.

I felt the car jolt and heard the sickening sound of buckling metal and shattering glass as the car rolled over onto the roof. Sitting there upside down, I thought *Oh shit, Big Ed is going to kill me.*

We were saved by the fact that I hadn't been going very fast. We crawled out of the driver side window, her pulling up her stockings, me trying to button my pants. That's when I realized my left hand, which had fallen out of the driver's window, couldn't move. It was embedded with glass.

As we were trying to get ourselves together and look decent, a guy came ruining up to us and asked, "What happened did a dog run in front of you or something?"

Wow, what a great idea!

"Yes, yes a dog ran right in front of us," I said. "I hit he breaks and the car pulled to the right and hit this parked car."

An ambulance pulled up to take us to the hospital. No cops. Thank God, because I was stinking drunk.

At the hospital, I saw the same ER doctor that I'd seen just the week before. I was a frequent flier. He wrapped my left hand in a cast. Yep, I'd broken that one too.

Sitting in the ER at 7 a.m., my new girlfriend called her boyfriend to come pick her up.

Over six-foot tall and at least two hundred and fifty pounds, he had the aura of a hit man. Later I found out he was Joe Conforte's bodyguard.

Joe Conforte was the owner of the world-famous Mustang Ranch, a legal brothel a few miles out of Reno. In other words, her boyfriend was not a very kind man. His eyes burned through me like a cutting torch. I breathed a sigh of relief when they left without incident.

Now it was my turn to call Mom and let her know I couldn't make it to Fallon for Mother's Day. With a cast on each hand, I couldn't drive.

Big Ed was making a killing buying custom trucks and cars from Texas. Because of the big oil squeeze, many people were selling their assets. These autos were pimped out with features like ice boxes between the Mastercraft seats and crush velvet upholstery. They featured gleaming paint, expensive rims and tires, and custom stereos.

I had to take some time off from driving and from the salon because of my hands. But I still did hair at my home. I wiggled my hands out of the casts to do this, although I could not wrap perms because that took too much dexterity. Finally, the doctor removed both casts. We would deliver a car and pick one or two cars up. Or I would drive my screaming VW Rabbit Diesel to the car lot and pick up my cars or trucks and tow the Rabbit back. I had been doing this for a year or so off and on for extra cash.

I started to accumulate speeding tickets. It seemed as though I could not make a trip without accruing many tickets. It seemed odd. I'd spent a lot of years speeding and until recently had never gotten caught.

Many trips were to Beaverton, Oregon, a twenty-hours round trip. I'd drive, sleep four hours, and do it again. Three trips a week.

Once, at about 3 a.m. on my way home I saw a huge wolf running alongside of me on the side of the road. I thought *I sure hope he doesn't run in front of me.* He looked over at me, his great piercing eyes hitting mine. At that very second he ran right in front of the car, almost rolling me. It was as though I had hit a cow. I had to pull over for a breather.

Dave was a little wild, yet nothing like his brothers Teddy and Rodd. Blond and about five feet ten, Rodd was a third degree black belt and loved to fight and often did. And now he's doing life for murder. Teddy was same height as Rodd, but built much heavier, weighing in around 250 pounds. Just like Rodd, he was always looking for a fight. And just like Rodd, he's in prison doing twenty to life for his third strike.

Teddy and I did not see eye to eye. Once we even broke out into a fist fight at 3 a.m. in Klamath Falls on Main Street. A bus drove by and people cheered out the window at us. This was not how it was supposed to be. Even if we could not be friends, we at least needed to be colleagues who could peacefully drive a car.

"Hey Big Ed," I said after the Klamath Falls debacle. "Please don't send Little Teddy and me out on jobs together. Someone is going to get hurt."

"Okay," he said. "But I have just one more job for you guys I need you to do."

If I had known what was to come of this job, I would have never gone.

The job was to drive the Rabbit down to Ontario, California and pick up four trucks to drive back. We brought along Dick, who was Teddy's girlfriend's little brother, and my friend Chris. I had a traffic court appearance for speeding the next day in Reno. I figured we could drive there, pick up the trucks and then bring them back in time for me to make court. I thought I was Superman.

When we hit Ontario, we discovered one truck was still in the upholstery shop and would not be done until the next day, and another would not be ready until 8 p.m.

I called my old roommate Martin and told him I was in Ontario, and had a few hours to kill. We agreed to meet at our old sushi bar. I had not had sushi since I moved back to Reno. I was craving it.

The guys told me they would have dinner and drinks at the Hilton. Little Teddy had his dad's credit card and I was to meet them in the parking lot at 11p.m. That would give us enough time to get back and me to court.

At 11 p.m., I was knocking on the window of the truck in the Hilton parking lot. Dick rolled down the window. I could see Teddy was passed out. Just like him. He was always drinking like a fiend whenever he had access to dad's credit cards.

"Listen, Dick," I said. "I have to leave; I have court at 9 a.m. We have to come back and pick up one truck tomorrow. If you want to follow me then do it. Obviously, Little Teddy can't drive right now."

We hauled ass, averaging 90 MPH, to a place called Four Corners. Coming out of Southern California where two highways meet, one to Barstow and one to Los Angeles, we were one hundred miles from where I lost my thumb and almost lost my life. Four Corners had a gas station on each corner where I always stopped for fuel. It was now 2:30 a.m. and we were a good six hours from Reno. As I was pumping gas, I wondered if I'd make it to court on time.

Next thing I knew, like a rabid animal, Little Teddy jumped on me and started pummeling me.

"You are not the boss!" he screamed. "My dad is the boss. You do not make the decisions, my dad does!"

I'd had enough of this asshole. An undefeated wrestler for many years, I didn't like hurting people, but I knew what I had to do. I reached to grab him by the shoulders so I could shove his ass right through the fuel pump.

These were the old style fuel pumps that had a glass window over the front of the machine; the numbers rolled behind the glass. I was furious. I wanted his blood. As I grabbed his shoulders to push him, my right hand slipped off his shoulder. And then my hand and forearm went through the glass and out the other side of the fuel pump.

Pain surged through me. It felt like I was being electrocuted. I wasn't sure if it was electric shock from the electricity in the pump, or the electric shock you feel when you touch your bare exposed nerves to cold metal.

When I pulled my arm out of the razor sharp glass, I could see both bones from wrist to elbow. The insides hung out, looking like a tri-tip. At that moment, it struck me *I'm in the middle of nowhere at 2:30 a.m. I am a dead motherfucker.*

Teddy kept trying to grab my arm and fight. I was hitting him with my left hand now, blood gushing out of my right arm. Finally, the attendant came out with baseball bat, acting like he was going to take Little Teddy's head off.

"If you make one more move," the attendant yelled, "I will smash your head like a pumpkin!"

I was lying in a pool of blood. I could smell the tang of iron in the blood. It was difficult to stay awake. I could feel the blood exiting my body rapidly; I shivered with cold.

Chris started tearing everyone's belts off, and tied three tourniquets around my upper right arm trying to slow the bleeding.

The horror of my drilling rig accident came racing back to me.

Death Valley, I thought, *you got me anyway.*

The pool of blood grew along with the stench of iron. I plead with God, *you would not do this to me again, would you? I know you are not a cruel Lord. Is this my karma?*

Now it was time to sleep. I couldn't keep awake or warm any longer; I was frozen to the bone.

The next thing I knew, a doctor in the E.R. was reaching into my arm to clamp the arteries. It felt like he was sticking a 220-volt wire into my arm. It was electrocuting me. I was in so much pain and shock I started to punch the doctor in the face.

"Put him out before it's too late!" he yelled.

I woke up in a hospital bed the next morning in Barstow. My right hand was in a cast so big you couldn't see the outline of a hand.

I didn't make it to court. Worse yet, Dr. McCuskey informed me I might lose my right hand. I had no insurance. One of a kind, Dr. McCuskey said he'd do the surgeries for me without payment or insurance. Yet he told me he would rather see me get insurance and consult with his friend Dr. Brown, a hand surgeon specialist in San Francisco's Presbyterian hospital who was one of the best in the country.

Why had I moved back to Reno? It seemed to bring out the brutality in me. All these crazy, fighting, hard drinking, fast driving, testosterone-driven fiends, and I became one of them. In Southern California doing hair, I'd been Warren Beatty, ladies' man, and charming hairstylist. In Reno, I was a beast.

Chapter 4: Wild Rides

"Can you please zip my pants up?" I shyly asked my date.

I was standing there at the dinner table with my right hand encased in an immense cast. Lori, a beautiful brown-eyed Italian girl with long dark naturally curly hair, and I were on our first date at the Glory Hole, a steak house. I laughingly explained to her that I had to divulge a secret: I could not zip my zipper with my right hand completely covered and only four digits on my left hand. And I needed to use the rest room. She promptly got up and escorted me to the bathroom, waiting for me just outside the door. When I came out of the bathroom, while zipping my pants up, she caressed my crotch and leaned into me, giving me a wet kiss. I had a feeling I might get lucky that night. When we left the restaurant later that evening we started a heated affair that was pure passion and lasted for many months.

While getting girls to zip up my pants was an advantage, my medical situation was mostly a hot mess. Big Ed's partner in the car lot, Mr. Klink, said he hoped I had good insurance because I was self-contracted. Mr. Klink was a stern guy in his late forties or early fifties; we called him Colonel Klink. He informed me that his company was not responsible.

I talked to an attorney who said that because the car lot had given me paychecks for hourly wages, they were responsible. While we could bring suit, they could liquidate their assets, and we could end up with nothing. He insisted that I try my best to get Big Ed and Mr. Klink to put me on the industrial insurance. At least that way I would be able to start to see the hand surgeon specialist.

After one phone call from the attorney, Big Ed came knocking at the screen door. Dave, Big Ed's son and my best friend, once told me that when Big Ed is sweating on his upper lip, that means he is very stressed and if he is sweating from his upper and lower lips he's about to go off. Known as the Mill Street Gorilla, Big Ed didn't get that name for wearing a gorilla suit. He got that name because he would bust your head if you pissed him off. A good size man, the Mill Street Gorilla stood nearly six feet tall and had impressive shoulders and big gnarly hands. He was a gruff man and he did not beat around the bush. I think that is why he made such a good wholesaler. Everyone respected him and most feared him.

When I answered the knock at the screen door, I felt the summer heat and saw Big Ed's sweaty upper lip. Nervousness flowed through my body.

"Hey buddy, how're you doing?" asked Big Ed.

We stood outside in the sun, so we were both sweating now.

"Oh, I've been better, Big Ed," I said.

"I can see that, buddy. What a shame this happened."

Was he genuinely concerned? Or was he playing me? I had warned him not to send Little Teddy and me out on any more jobs together. I had told him someone was going to get hurt. But he was sweating on the upper lip, so I didn't dare say that.

"Listen, Cliff. There is no way in hell I'm going to lose my car lot and livelihood over this."

His gorilla countenance loomed over me. Was he going to hit me? Could I take him, with my cast? My body prickled with perspiration.

"So," he continued. "I'm going to get you on industrial insurance."

I exhaled. Thank God.

Over the next few months, Dr. Brown performed two surgeries. An older gentleman, a little portly and very kind, Dr. Brown had a good bedside manner. He always said hi and asked how I was doing. He listened to me well and took all my questions seriously.

My right hand was basically what they called a claw. I had no dexterity and couldn't extend my fingers. The fuel pump had sliced my muscles, tendons, nerves, veins and arteries like a meat slicer, lengthwise up my arm. When I'd pulled my right arm out of the fuel pump, the ulna and radial bones were revealed from wrist to elbow. Because of the nature of the injury, I was developing massive amounts of scar tissue up and down the length of my arm. We were going to try muscle, tendon, and nerve grafts.

On the day of surgery, I checked into Pacific Presbyterian Hospital. Sitting in the waiting room, I took note of the bright lights and shiny floors, the gleaming counters. People efficiently bustled about. Compared to the dreary old Washoe Medical back in Reno, this felt more like a business office than a hospital.

I had driven myself here in my faded silver 1976 280Z, a four speed with stick shift. It could go 160 MPH and still get thirty-five miles to the gallon. Because it was a three and half hour drive from Reno to San Francisco, I didn't ask anyone to take me to the hospital. I didn't want to in inconvenience anyone. Besides, no one liked California traffic.

Crossing the Bay Bridge made me uneasy. I hated heights. From there, I proceeded to the Embarcadero and then winded through the streets of Chinatown. The air smelled of the sea and the sweet eucalyptus trees. Expertly grabbing at the clutch, I negotiated San Francisco's famously steep hills.

Soon, I was checked into my room. Surgery would be performed at 6 a.m., a nerve graft from my left calf to my right forearm. I really had not given it much thought. As far as I was concerned it was just another surgery followed by a two-week stay on a serve-yourself morphine pump. Having gone through so many surgeries, I knew to insist on a lot of pain meds. Those little grafts hurt like hell. When I told the doctor I didn't want to feel any pain, he winked back at me, an assurance I'd be plied with meds.

Surgery lasted twelve hours. When I was taken back to my room I hit the button on my pain pump. They had it set so high that it doused me like a wave. I almost vomited, but kept it down with little swallows.

For the two weeks after these surgeries I mostly slept although sometimes I would be able to get up and smoke a joint. Weed helped with the nausea from the morphine.

One afternoon I was sitting on the ledge of the window smoking a joint. Suddenly the nurse came in. Her face contorted with anger. *Busted.*

"Oh my God, get away from that window!" she yelled. "Do you want to fall out?"

She didn't care I was smoking the joint. She just didn't want me to sit at the window on the fifth floor, obviously high on morphine.

I was anxious to get outside, to feel the sun on my face and smell the fresh salty air. I couldn't wait to get home and sleep in my own bed. Dr. Brown ordered a shot of morphine for me for the ride home. He knew I had a four-hour ride. I don't think he knew I was driving myself.

I used crutches to get to the car. By the time I got to the parking lot, I was sweating profusely, out of shape from lying down being pumped full of morphine for two weeks.

I stared at the stick shift and clutch. Wait a minute, I had a cast from my hip to my ankle on my left leg, and a bent-arm cast on my right arm. My whole hand was covered; you couldn't even see my fingers.

I was four hours from home and had a forty-five-minute drive through the city, through Chinatown and up and down all those hills. How in the hell was I going to drive?

After stuffing myself into the cockpit of the tiny car, I threw my crutches in the back. I reached over with my left hand to find and turn the key and start the car. My fuel-injected beauty had a high idle and ran great! Great White blasted out the speakers.

I sat there thinking. *Should I turn the car off and call someone? No, I just couldn't. I had to do this on my own.*

Reaching over with my left hand, I grabbed the stick shift. Stretching my right foot over, I pushed in the clutch. With my left hand I put the car in reverse then let the clutch out. I carefully backed up. Then I put the car into first gear with my left hand and released the clutch with my right foot.

It was working.

As I got going I shifted to second. First and second would get me through the city. With my window down the fresh sea air cooled off my sweaty body.

Suddenly I had to stop on a severe incline. *Shit.* I jumped from the break to the clutch with my right foot and at the same time reached over with my left hand and hit first gear. Simultaneously, I let the clutch out and stood on the gas with the right foot so the car wouldn't roll back.

I thought getting home would be the end of it. But little did I know I had something even harder to face: cold turkey.

After four hours at home, the two weeks of morphine started to wear thin. I couldn't lie down; I couldn't stand up. It was as though I could not stand being in my own body. I felt like I wanted to throw my guts up and out of the universe.

At the same time, it was like I had pissed off a gang of badasses who'd pummeled me with two-by-fours. My sides and back were ached with excruciating pain. It hurt to breathe like I had broken ribs.

Finally, I called the doctor.

"You're going through withdrawals," he said. He informed me there was not much I could do about it other than get hooked on morphine. It was a do or die situation. "You either kick it now and control yourself. Or let the drug control you."

For the next surgery, I insisted on Demerol.

I had to learn how to navigate life with the use of only a thumb-less left hand. I'd walk out of the bathroom with many pieces of paper stuck to my face the first few times after shaving. Or ram the toothbrush down the back of my throat while brushing my teeth. Buttoning my shirt was agonizing. And forget about multi-tasking.

But what could I do? Stop living?

That was never in the cards for me; I just plugged away and focused on the few simple benefits. "Excuse me, can you please help zip up my pants?"

Chapter 5: Set Up

A little over a year had passed since the fuel pump incident. I couldn't open my right hand although I was right-handed. Talk about physically and emotionally stressful. Growing up I was always active. I use to buck hay, ride horses and bulls and play football. I was undefeated in wrestling, and I crashed many motorcycles. Now I was embarrassed to put out my right hand to shake someone's hand. Instead I offered my left. Most people went along and just reached out to my left. Some of my friends, though, insisted on shaking my right hand.

I had several more surgeries, including one where Dr. Brown fused my right thumb at a 90-degree angle, an attempt to bring some kind of function to my hand.

With my thumb at a 90-degree angle I should have been able to grasp a pencil or some small object between my thumb and index finger. I still had no feeling in my arm or hand. There were times when I was barbecuing and happened to look down, only to realize I had grilled myself.

Dr. Brown said I should consider having the right hand removed, and replaced with a prosthetic hand or even a hook. I couldn't get my head wrapped around this. A boy in my elementary school who had lost a hand had a hook. I thought how unfortunate he was, how cold and machine-like it looked. Yet, it didn't seem to bother him. But me? I just couldn't see myself that way.

My ego was not going to allow me to have a missing hand. I told Dr. Brown I refused both of these options instead would rebuild myself with weights. Like I had done with my left hand and arm, I could tie the weights to my hands and wrists and rehabilitate myself.

At age twenty-three, having undergone so much bodily destruction and pain, I just wanted to forget about it and have a good time. I was taking Darvocet, an opioid pain killer that eventually got banned due to side effects. I was also taking Flexeril for the daily muscle spasms; I could sit and watch as the muscles in my right forearm jumped involuntarily. I was also taking Halcion, a sleeping pill that has many side effects including increased anger and the aggravation of pins and needles sensations.

Most of the drugs I avoided taking because I didn't like feeling constantly hung over. But the Darvocet I did take regularly to alleviate the constant pain.

For shits and giggles I would put a Flexeril into my roommate's beers for the hell of it every now and then. Kenny, a very skilled painter who had helped me restore my '59 Ford, never realized what I had done.

When he was having trouble walking and talking, I would tell him what I did. We would just laugh it off. At the time I didn't think about how I was putting people in jeopardy. Later, a lawyer would argue my actions were due to "diminished capacity" from so many drugs.

On top of my prescription drugs, I enjoyed a little smoke and a little drink. I'd discovered at an early age that buying a big enough bag of weed meant I could sell some and get mine for free. I was making

$606.66 every two weeks on disability. What an odd number. Did the Devil calculate it?

I partied a lot with my roommates Chief and Little Chief, brothers of Native American and Danish heritage, as well as our friend Jeff Tally. They had a friend named Butch, who lived by Cal Expo in Sacramento, a big man who often took steroids while playing football for Sacramento City College. A powerful man with a strong personality, Butch was dating a woman named Peggy…his best friend's mother. Butch was not into recreational drugs. I don't think he even drank. One day when he was up visiting Peggy from Sacramento, he told us his roommate Howard could get cocaine for $600 an ounce, $2,400 for a quarter pound. We weren't interested. We called coke *S'mores* because once you started you wanted Some More. Who needed that monkey on his back?

Instead, my focus was my '76 280Z. I wanted to paint it black to match my '59 Ford pickup I had just prepared for Hot August Nights. The Z was scary. It would do 160 MPH no sweat. I had low pro-rims and tires mounted along with life time guarantee racing struts for stability. It had a nice stereo and just needed a nice black paint job.

Worm, who worked at an auto detail and accessory shop, helped me finish my truck, doing the upholstery and window tinting. Worm was very pale, which made his dark brown hair, parted on the side, stand out. To get the paint perfect Kenny and I prepped and sanded for hours. Then came the chroming of the glove box, ashtray and the windshield defroster band. I chromed the glove box because I dug the chrome glove box from the movie "American Graffiti" that allowed you to look up the skirts of your date.

We had good times working on this truck. Sometimes we just sat around and drank many beers. Sometimes we would do an occasional mushroom or two, and we always smoked a lot of pot.

One day Worm asked me if I knew where he could get some coke. His brother-in-law was working at the mines in Northern

Nevada. There, he sold coke and earned a lot of money. Remembering Butch's roommate Howard, I said I could probably get a couple grams for two hundred and fifty bucks.

"No, man," he laughed. "I want more like an ounce or two."

"Oh," I said. That sounded scary. "Nah, I don't want to get involved with amounts like that."

A couple days later, Worm called me, telling me his brother-in-law said he would give us $2,400 for two ounces. I vaguely wondered why he kept calling me for this but then I calculated that I'd make $1,200 profit fast. For doing almost nothing. I figured I'd drive to Sacramento, pick up the coke from Butch then come back to Reno where Worm would accompany me to Lovelock to meet his brother-in-law.

I was ready. The Z car would be our 160 MPH chariot that got 35 miles to the gallon.

Butch agreed to front me a couple of ounces. We set the times and dates. Right as I was stepping out the door to leave, Worm called.

"Hey, man," he said. "I've got a shit load of tint jobs to do and I just can't make it. You know the drill right? My brother-in-law is expecting you. I told him I can't make it. No biggie, he is a nice guy, you'll like him."

An odd bolt of lightning shot through my gut. Was Worm playing me? Was he actually scared to go? But I dismissed the feeling, focusing on the money. Maybe with my new funds I could paint the Z car.

As I was flying through the Sierras in the Z, I was trying not to think about the drugs. Instead, I thought about driving, how my best friend Big Dave, a sprint car racer, taught me that when you hit the corners high they shoot you out low. Most people hit the corners low and wonder why it shoots them to the top. Hitting some corners at 100-120 MPH, I was amazed at how the physics worked. Hitting the corner just right sets you up for the next corner. It made me excited to drive fast, the adrenaline flowed; I loved my car.

As I approached Butch's house I couldn't help but notice, there must have been about twelve pairs of sneakers on his porch. They were all thrown in a pile: white, blue, red, Pumas, Nikes, Asics, used and worn out. It looked like a lost and found. Yet they all seemed to be one size: huge. And all the soles looked worn and clean.

Howard opened the door and invited me in. He and Butch were the only two at the apartment. Howard was a monster of a man, at least six foot six. He seemed reserved until he spouted off, "We know where you live." *Was there a hint of a real threat in that joke?* He had a big shit-eating grin.

Laughingly, I replied, "Darn, I hoped Butch had forgotten. I will have the money back to you in two days."

"No problem," Howard said. "I'm not worried about it. Butch will pay for you if you don't." He laughed again.

Howard then informed me it would take about two hours for him to go and retrieve the coke. Since it would take a while for the goods to arrive, Butch suggested a little fishing. So we grabbed poles and a tackle box. Then the mystery of the shoes was answered, as Butch slid his bare feet into a pair of the shoes, "Ah, a dry pair, these are my river shoes I use for fishing."

The river was only a fifteen-minute walk from the apartment. Within a few minutes we stood on the beach of the American River. Huge cottonwoods and willows lined the banks. The water was high and a bluish-green, the sandy beaches a nice break from the concrete and pavement just yards away. We found a nice spot in the shade with access to the water through the trees. The breeze felt cool on our shoulders. Butch tied a piece of red yarn to a hook, added some weights and cast her in.

Bam! Something took the hook. Butch had his hands full for a few moments. It was a good fight and we could tell it would be good sized fish. Within minutes he had landed a nice Shad, twenty-four inches long and weighing in at about ten pounds. Checking out a few more of

Butch's lucky fishing holes, we caught a few more fish.

When we got back to the house, Howard had arrived with the goods. We sat at the table in the kitchen as Howard pulled the coke out of a brown paper bag. He laid two plastic bags on the table. It was the most cocaine I had ever seen, it was white with a yellowish hue. Big chunks, very little duff or powder. Which meant it was good and pure, not all powder and full of cut.

At that moment I was flushed with fear and started to sweat, finally realizing, *that's a lot of cocaine.*

When it was time to go, I put the coke in the bag and stuffed it down my pants. Nervously, I walked to my car and took the back off of one of my speakers and stuffed the bag in.

As I drove, my skin was crawling. I was so anxious I could barely breathe. The sweat was pouring off me. I watched the speedometer, not going a mile over sixty. It was the longest trip from Sacramento to Reno I ever made.

The next morning I awoke with a knot in my stomach. I didn't want to go through with taking the coke to Lovelock, about two-and-a-half hours north east of Reno. I would be driving through the barest of deserts. Nothing to look at but sand and sagebrush. Maybe a cow skull here and there or some salt flats. The air so dry, it dehydrated your sinuses. But what could I do? Return it to monstrous Howard? Guys like that usually frown upon such moves.

I'm not sure why I asked my best friend Joe if he wanted to come for a ride to Lovelock with me. Maybe for the comfort, to reassure myself. After all, he'd been my friend since middle school. Joe graduated from University of Nevada, Reno with a degree in business and had just set up an interview for a new job. Even though he was not thrilled with the position, he had a lot going for him. He had finally graduated college after many years of school, along with recently landing his high school crush, whom he had wanted to catch for many years. Joe was finally getting his life together.

"Hey Joe, what are you doing today?" I asked.

"Nothing much," he replied.

"I have to go to Lovelock and make a drop off to Worm's brother-in-law. I am meeting him at the KOA in a few hours."

"Sounds fun, you buying?" he asked.

"Sure, how about steak and lobster at the Sturgeon?"

"Come get me," he said.

The whole way to Lovelock I obeyed the speed limit. The plan was to meet John David Black, Worm's brother-in-law, at the KOA campground just on the east side of Lovelock. Lovelock is a one-horse town that takes all of five minutes to drive through. The KOA was tiny, maybe ten RV parking places. I knew we would easily see John David's red Fierro. He was supposed to bring a six-pack of beer to enjoy.

When we pulled in the campground my nerves were frazzled. I had been on pure adrenaline for over twenty-four hours now. We crept past a few rundown trailers, a small store, a Laundromat, a few water stained sheds that were barely standing. As we passed some trees, we saw John David leaning against his red car. Tall with blond curly hair, he greeted us with a big smile and a handshake. I handed him the bundle, sweat prickling my back as I imagined him pulling out handcuffs. Instead he opened the package and put his finger in one of the plastic bags and tasted it.

"How about a pound?" he asked, a big smile on his face.

A pound? Fuck no! I only did this to help Worm out. And to get some quick cash. But no way, not a pound.

"I don't want to get into big amounts." I said.

"No problem, I understand," John David replied.

It was hot out. The ice cold beer felt good running down the back of my throat, and with not much food in my stomach, I felt the effects of the alcohol immediately. With very little chitchat John David counted out $2,400 in cash and handed it to me. I stuffed it far down in my front pocket as I crawled back into the Z car.

As we headed out of the KOA, I had a nervous feeling we would be pulled over and arrested. When we finally made it to the restaurant, relief washed over me.

Joe and I ordered lobster and steak, medium rare. But when the food came, I didn't have much of an appetite. I took a bite. No flavor.

As I sat there in the 1950s style booth, exhaustion hit me like a flood. There was a well-worn checkerboard pattern tile floor beneath my feet and an old jukebox in the corner playing Hank Williams Jr., "Whiskey Bent and Hell Bound." The old dusty clock on the wall seemed to barely be clicking away. For a moment I felt like I was dreaming, like time was standing still.

"You ready?" Joe asked.

I woke out of my daze.

"Let's make like babies and head out," I said

The trip home, we hauled ass. We had nothing to fear but a speeding ticket.

Chapter 6: Busted

It was as exciting as Christmas morning counting my money on the living room floor. There was roughly $4,000: $12,000 from John David Black, along with some other funds I had put away.

I gave my roommate Chief a couple hundred dollars to help him and his brother out. They were struggling to start their own cabinet business. Their shop was our garage, and there was never a time when they didn't have it filled with cabinets, saw dust, empty beer bottles and sometimes deer hanging from the rafters. As Native Americans, they could shoot as many deer in a year as they needed. Chief and Little Chief would usually get a couple of deer, one for the three of us and one I would make into deer jerky for our families.

It was early August and I was looking forward to Hot August Nights, one of the largest classic auto shows on the West Coast. There would be thousands of classic cars roaming the streets of Reno and Lake Tahoe, Nevada. Events ranged from poker runs and contests where contestants see who can make the longest burn out with their car. There were also concerts by such bands as The Beach Boys, sock hops and classic car auctions.

I'd worked on my midnight black '59 Ford truck for many years, and now she was going to be ready to play at Hot August Nights. Kenny got the paint so straight, Lake Tahoe reflected off her as if in a mirror.

Lifted with massive tires, the truck was easily powered by a high performance 390. It had gorgeous burgundy and gray crushed velvet interior.

I'd recently bought my roommate's black jet boat and now I wanted to paint my Z car black to match. I loved black shine.

I planned to go to school to become an x-ray or ultrasound technician. With that career, I'd be able to buy all the toys I wanted. And then a house. It would be a good life. Little did I know God hadn't read the same play book I had.

A few days before Hot August Nights, the phone rang.

"Hey, Cliff, how's it going?"

It took me a minute to recognize John David Black's voice. Once I did, I had wished I hadn't answered the phone. If there was ever a time for screening a call this was it. I already knew why he was calling. I wasn't interested; I thought I had made that clear. Just the sound of his voice made my blood pressure rise and me nervous.

"Hey, what's going on John David?" I replied.

"I was wondering, Cliff, if you had given it much thought to what I had asked you in Lovelock?"

"Not really John David, I told you I don't want to do that large of a quantity," I said nervously.

"I will pay you $8,000 for a half pound."

"I don't know, I'm really uncomfortable. Let me think about it."

His offer meant I could make thirty-two hundred bucks in a couple days. I could easily afford to get the Z painted then. Then that

would sleep for the entire weekend not moving a muscle.

Other guys I knew, like the car lot owners I wholesaled cars to who made $20,000 a month or more, did a lot of blow. I saw them smoke it, snort it, eat it, you name it. So I knew first hand we had some pure cocaine and we could easily cut an ounce out of eight ounces and no one would complain. A way to milk as much money as possible out of this last deal.

The next morning dawned hot, as usual in Reno in August. I was sick with nerves. In shorts and a tank top, I threw my sandals in the back of the Z. Worm rode shotgun as I stayed at the speed limit on the road to Lovelock, the package tucked away under Worm's seat.

I had history with Lovelock. My nephew's father came from there, and his grandmother use to serve as a judge. And here I was driving to that town with a half-pound of coke.

Thirty minutes outside of Reno I pulled over in Fernley to buy a Big Gulp. No way was I going to drink it; I was so nervous I couldn't keep down food or drink. I just needed a cup and some anti-freeze.

"Here," I said handing Worm the cup, "throw the drink out the window. Now take the foil off of the top of the anti-freeze."

I continued to direct him to wipe the cup out with a rag, take the coke out of the bag and put in the cup. I really thought I had the situation handled.

"Why are we doing this?" Worm asked.

"If anything, and I mean anything, looks suspicious or goes wrong, you pour the antifreeze on the coke and throw it out the window I will worry about getting the money back to them later."

"Are you scared?"

"Hell, yes, I'm scared," I said, wondering why he asked me this question. I figured If John David were a cop, he would have busted me the last time.

Still my mind raced. Something seemed strange. Was John David really Worm's brother-in-law? Why would he ask me about my state of mind? Shouldn't this be cut and dried?

As we entered Lovelock, a cop car was parked right next to the first gas station on the main street. A rock hard lump stuck in my throat. I just wanted to get this the hell over with.

When we got to the other end of the one-horse town, we saw another cop car, this one driving towards town. My fingers trembled on the steering wheel. My intuition was flaring up like a house on fire. Should I go through with this? *No*, said my intuition. *Haul ass out of town.*

My heart was pounding so hard it was ringing in my ears.

"Pour the antifreeze on the coke!" I yelled.

"What?" Worm asked.

"Pour the fucking antifreeze on the coke."

He just sat there, holding the cup. At that moment, John David Black's little red car rode under the overpass we were on. I took a breath. Maybe I was overreacting. Still I just wanted to get this the fuck over with.

"Let's go." I said.

We pulled up to the meeting spot, the parking lot of Sturgeons, the run down restaurant and motel where Joe and I had stopped to eat on the previous trip.

As we pulled up I immediately notice John David had another person in his car with him. A pale man with dark brown hair, cut short, like a cop would wear. I tried to push my fear down deep into my stomach. This wasn't worth it. But it was too late to back out now.

I got out of the car. The asphalt was hot on my bare feet. John David introduced me to the pale man: Steve.

"You have no shoes," Steve said.

"Am I going to need them?" I half-joked, trying unsuccessfully to ease the panic rushing through my veins.

Worm and John David went around the back of my car to exchange the coke for the cash. Out of the motel window came a whistle. A woman's whistle. Once. Twice. And then a blue Ford Bronco cruised into the parking lot, straight towards us. In a split second I saw a cop in uniform was the driver.

The motel doors flew open. At least ten cops poured out, holding their guns.

The Bronco skidded to a stop and the cop leaped out, gun in hand.

"Get down! Put your hands behind your back! Now! Get down!"

Everything shifted into slow motion, like there was extra space between each second. My limbs moved like I was in water.

As I dropped to my knees, I saw John David and Steve had pulled their guns too. Somehow, deep down, I was not surprised. But then I saw Worm standing next to John David, like they were buddies.

"You better get down too Worm," John David said. As if to say, just *get down and play along*.

I could barely breathe. I'd been set up. The slow-motion feeling vanished and now the world was twirling around me like I was on a fast spinning merry-go-around.

After cuffing me, cops were yelling to get up on my feet, yanking on the cuffs to hoist me up. The hand cuffs were so tight, they bit into my wrists and my fingers went numb. As the cops read us our rights, all I heard was mumbo jumbo over the buzzing in my ears from the blood rushing through head. Then they told us to watch our heads as they loaded Worm and me into the cop car.

The ride to the jail-house was just a few minutes, but it was excruciating. I couldn't seem to gather my thoughts. I was suffocating, soaked in sweat. How would I tell my parents I'd been arrested? There was no way in hell I could. I just did not have the heart. I figured I would have to call my sister. How humiliating.

A cop held my elbow out of the car. He was a little guy, but I was cuffed. I wanted to run, but there was nothing I could do.

"If I run, will you shoot me?" I asked.

He looked at me. "What?"

"I can't call my family and tell them what just happened," I said. "Will you shoot me?"

"No," he said. "Just tackle you. And then charge you with attempted escape.

Chapter 7: Out of my Element

This must be how a wild animal feels locked up.

The gray brick cell had no windows. There were gray bars to match. In a green jumpsuit with plastic shower shoes, I was stuck with four other guys: two gray haired older guys, and two closer to my age. The clanking of metal bar doors and gates echoed across the concrete floors as the police opened and closed the doors.

In the corner, a small black and white TV showed Andy and Barney in Mayberry, a fantasy-land where jail was a joke. A dank unclean smell permeated the air, which was thick with cigarette smoke. A stainless steel sink-toilet combo lurked in the corner.

It was the morning after the bust. My friends had expected me back by seven p.m. What were they thinking?

That night I hadn't slept, with my mind racing, wondering what the hell I was going to do. After I had called my sister and spent a couple hours in a holding tank, the police put me in a cell all alone, no chairs no tables, just an empty brick room. Ten minutes later John David Black walked in. Unlike the smiling, fun guy he had played previously, he was very serious and red in the face. With his button-up shirt, bolo tie, jeans and cowboy boots, he was trying for the urban cowboy look, but his long blond Mullet betrayed him.

"Didn't your gut feelings tell you something wrong was going on?" he asked.

"Yes," I admitted.

"You should learn to listen to your gut feelings," he said. "I'm an undercover agent for the Nevada Division of Investigation. We want your connection. We will give you the money for this buy and set up another deal. If you work with us, you get off with probation. If not, you're looking at forty years in prison for trafficking this amount."

The room spun. I felt like I was slowly being deflated, deprived of oxygen. I wanted to vomit. Forty years? How old would I be in forty years? I couldn't wrap my mind around it. I was still trying to fathom what just happened, and why Worm picked me to set up.

I knew I couldn't turn in Butch. No matter what bad shit I had pulled, I was *not* a rat. *Can't do the time, don't do the crime,* played over and over in my head.

Wasn't I better than this? A fire that burned constantly deep inside my gut. It told me never to quit. Never give up. I had applied it to football and wrestling and art. I would actually picture myself winning my matches in my mind, or making plays in football, and get a rush of adrenaline. Yet I had failed to apply this fire, this focus, to education, to moral choices, to my future. I was disgusted with myself. I'd had bigger and better dreams than going to prison at age twenty-three.

"Who is Joe?" said John David Black. "And where is he?"

Oh, God. Joe. Why did they want him?

"Just a friend. I swear he had no idea what was going on," I said.

"He is looking at aiding and abetting for accompanying you on the drop off of the first two ounces."

"He had no fucking idea what I was doing," I said, looking John David in the eye. I told him I would buy him steak and lobster if he went along for a ride."

"Is that so?" John David asked.

"Joe just graduated UNR. He is starting a new job and has his high school sweetheart. Please don't ruin his life for riding along with me. You have the person you set up. Leave Joe alone. Please."

"We'll soon know if what you are saying is true or not. We'll be raiding his house."

Oh shit, I hoped Joe and John had nothing at their home.

Like my near-death experience on the drilling rig, I felt my whole life rush right through me, but not my past, my future. I pictured myself old and gray coming out of the prison gates. I had been plucked from the monster jaws of a machine that almost killed me, and I survived a near fatal accident in a fight with a fuel pump… only to end up like this.

As the days went by, I ached with remorse and fear. At first, I couldn't eat the horrible food they served that was brought over from the hospital. Those poor patients. A couple of days later, I wasn't so picky.

I wondered what was going on with Worm. Was he in jail with me or not? I knew they didn't keep co-defendants in the same cell. This way they can be interrogated separately.

At the preliminary hearing, Worm was seated next to me at the table. He seemed nervous, pale and withdrawn. Dark rings circled his eyes. What the hell had he been thinking? I fumed with rage.

We were charged with trafficking of a controlled substance Level II. The hammer slammed down, bail set at $50,000 each.

My parents put up their ranch in Fallon for my bail. The place where I grew up, hunting in the meadows for quail, dove and pheasant. Picking lugs of peaches, cherries, and apples from the orchards. And of course bucking acres of hay.

And now they were picking me up from jail. I couldn't look at them. I kept my eyes down as I climb into the car. I felt empty but leaden.

From the back seat of the car, I stared at my father's neck, sunburned from working hay all day out in the fields or perhaps forty-eight hours of irrigating.

"Boy, you really did it this time." He said. "You have no education, and no hands. And now you have this hanging over your head."

Then he said something I didn't expect him to say on our conversation home.

"If they send you to prison, you better take advantage of every class or program they have."

"Yes, sir," I said, quietly, turning my head to the window. Sagebrush and sand flew by.

Chapter 8: Bail Out

On the first week I was out on bail after two weeks in the Lovelock jail, I savored the simple acts of showering and eating what I wanted when I wanted. The future played heavily on my mind. My body felt taxed and tired, weighed down by colossal emotions. I was irate with myself for letting Worm so easily talk me into this mess.

To add even more anguish, my mother called me with horrible news: Tana, who had been my first girlfriend, had been murdered. An Italian beauty, she had emerald green eyes and long wavy brown hair, she always had a tremendous smile on her beautiful face. Two years older than I, she babysat my nephew. I always liked older women. We spent many days together exploring each other's bodies and minds. I really missed her when my family moved from Washoe Valley to Fallon. I hadn't seen her in about eight years then we ran into each other at a Robert Plant concert just a few months back. I was shocked when I ran into her at first, not really knowing if it was her. After watching her for a moment I knew in my heart it was. She looked astonishing to me. She had her signature smile spread across her face and seemed just as happy to see me as I her.

She told me she was married and had two kids. Living in Carson City, she worked as a waitress in a steak house. She asked me to come see her at the restaurant. I did, a few times. As I walked out of the restaurant the last time, I never could have fathomed that in four months she'd be brutally murdered.

Getting this news was like being hit in the head with a baseball bat. I felt dizzy and nauseated, sickening feelings that lasted for days. A guy she was seeing on the side had murdered her. When her family was out of town on a camping trip, she had stayed behind to break things off with him. Rage-filled, he choked her to death. Then he went home and killed himself.

The second week out on bail I needed to see Dr. Brown about my right hand. On my way, I stopped in to see Butch. He and Howard had heard about my arrest. I wanted them to know I wouldn't rat them out. They seemed generally grateful. I explained to them in great detail everything that had happened.

"Hey man," I joked to Butch. "I will give twenty-five hundred dollars if you break John David's fucking legs."

"We could do that," Butch and Howard said, with big smiles and gleaming eyes.

"Or beat the fuck out of him and Worm." I could tell we'd shifted from joking to serious consideration.

"Could be arranged," Howard said.

"Let us think about it, we'll let you know."

Dr. Brown was still trying to convince me to replace my right hand with a hook. I wasn't ready for that step. I didn't tell him about being arrested, hoping I could beat this in court. Then he told me about another surgery he would like to try. It involved taking some tendons out of the back of my right hand and using them for graft surgery.

My third week out on bail, Butch came to Reno and invited me over to his girlfriend Peggy's house. He talked about a movie he just saw, *An Innocent Man* starring Tom Selleck.

"Don't go see it, dude," he said.

Of course I went. It's not pretty. Violence and rape in prison. And then Tom has to shank someone to save his own life. What a horrible feeling realizing that soon that film could me my real life.

After seeing the movie, I said to Butch, "Man I better start working out."

"If I was you, I'd start chemical war fare on your body and do some steroids. You can get big quick."

I agreed, he was right, I asked him to get me some.

"Well you know, the more we buy the better the price," he said.

"What do you mean? How much do we have to buy?" I asked, remembering that just a month ago after he shot me in the butt with some Decca to try. He'd said he could get me some for a hundred bucks.

"We need to purchase at least four or five hundred dollars' worth."

A funny feeling pulsed through me. This time I listened to my intuition.

"Sorry I'm broke" I said.

A day later, I got a call from my $10,000 attorney, the one I had to sell my '59 Ford truck to pay for.

"Get down to my office, pronto!" he yelled. "The court wants to revoke your bail." The thought of going back to that shithole in Lovelock curdled my blood.

In his big cherry wood and leather-upholstered chair behind his immense desk, the attorney glared at me. The blonde rug on his head may have matched his blond eyebrows, but it was askew and contrasted with his angry red face.

"What, do you want to go back to jail?"

"What do you mean?" I asked nervously.

"I just got a call from the Fucking D.A. He wants your ass now!"

"Why, what did I do?"

"The D.A. says he has evidence of you trying to put a hit out on John David Black, and that you are trying to purchase steroids. What the fuck are you doing? I told you not to talk to anyone involved."

I just sat there with a blank look on my face, my head twirling. Butch, the very son of a bitch I was bending over backwards to protect, was busy setting me up!

"You better get packed, they want you back in the Lovelock jail by three p.m. tomorrow."

Blood pounded in my ears. I reluctantly left his office to go pack up to turn myself in. Before I left for Lovelock, I made one last call to Butch.

"You're a fucking rat!" I yelled.

"What are you talking about?"

"I bent over backwards to protect you and you set me up?"

"I don't know what you're talking about, man."

"I'll see you in court, rat!" I slammed the phone down.

Filled with rage and confusion, I packed to check myself back in to Lovelock, realizing I couldn't trust anyone now.

On my way to jail, I thought about what my dad had said: Take advantage of every class and program they offer.

I also thought about a muscular guy with mousy brown hair I'd met last time in the cell. I wanted to know what prison was like.

"You'll learn how to survive there. It's bad, but if you mind your own business and program it will go by," he said.

"What do you mean by program?" I asked.

"If you want the time to go by, stay busy. Take classes, work out, just to keep yourself busy. It's not the time that is so bad, it's the people you have to spend time with."

Within two weeks of turning myself in, Dr. Brown sent a letter to the jail administration indicating I had to be in San Francisco for my medical check-ups every other week. Lovelock couldn't afford to take me back and forth to San Francisco for these weekly check-ups. So they volunteered my bail.

Even though I was having a lot of fun learning to smoke cigarettes and not get sick, I was thrilled to be out of there again. But I did not want to talk to or see anyone. I knew I couldn't trust a living soul.

Life seemed surreal. How could it be that I was out on bail for trafficking of a controlled schedule II substance? Was it karma for not really taking to heart the fact I had a Near Death Experience? I'd had a second chance at life, and I squandered it.

For the first year or two after my Near Death Experience I'd looked at life differently. I was very grateful for being alive and I felt an indescribable freshness. Nothing like I had felt since childhood. It was as though the slate had been wiped clean and I was starting over. I'd wanted to breathe and fill my lungs with as much clean air as possible. I'd wanted to learn, I craved knowledge and wanted to cram as much in as quickly as I could. But I never really learned to savor the moment. I was too unfocused, too thrown around by events, too filled with fire to sit still.

Maybe I was going through this time of difficulty because God was trying to get my attention again.

Out on bail for the second time from Lovelock, I'd been having a conversation with my brother-in-law Donnie on their porch,

"Hey Cliff," he said. "Have you been wearing those sunglasses I gave you this whole time? Your luck lately has been total shit and your life is going downhill."

What a strange question. And what was up with that look on his face?

"Yeah, I've been wearing them nonstop. Why?"

"I actually pulled those off of the driver of a fatal accident. The driver was dead when I had arrived on the scene of the roll-over accident with the tow truck."

Dread bolted through me like lightning. I couldn't believe what he was telling me.

I pulled the glasses off my head and stomped the lenses until they were crushed.

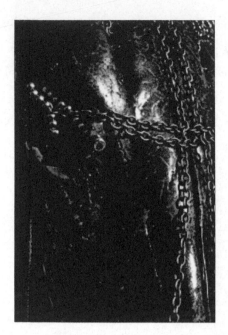

Chapter 9: Speak into the Microphone

For the second time I was released on bail from the Lovelock jail. Back home a week, I was listening to Great White cranked on my roommate's CD player. I had just walked in the house after smoking a joint outside in the back yard when I heard a knock on the door. It was 10:30 p.m. Who the hell would be showing up at this hour?

Two men stood on the front porch, one tall with short blond hair and one short and stocky with dark long hair. Behind them was parked an unmarked white police-style car. They flipped out their badges: Washoe County detectives.

"Michael Helm?"

"Yes, I'm Michael Helm, Why?"

"You're under arrest," the shorter one said.

"What do you mean? I'm out on bail. Why am I under arrest again?"

"What have you been doing that you shouldn't be?" asked the taller blond cop.

I wondered if they had just witnessed me out back smoking the joint.

"Nothing."

They placed the cuffs on me so tight my hands were numb in a matter of minutes. Now what is it going to be? Another bail out? Another couple months in county? Would this ever end? I had created one hell of a nightmare.

They marched me out and tossed me into the back of the unmarked cop car. Soon it became obvious we were not headed to the jail. Instead they drove out of Sparks about twelve miles east toward Mustang Ranch. My nerves pricked up. But I thought it might be better to stay quiet. I sat back and listened to them talk.

"Yeah," said the short cop, eying me in the rear-view mirror. "You should never try to put a hit out on a cop. Bad things can happen to you."

Was this about John David Black? Were these guys his buddies?

I started to sweat, contemplating what my immediate future was with my two new friends. My mind raced like a sprint car in the last turn, but I still kept quiet.

"There was no one home with you when we picked you up. So basically no one knows where you are or who you are with. We could put a bullet in your head and bury you in a shallow grave out here and no one would ever know."

I was a dead man.

They pulled over out by the Mustang Exit and parked a little distance from the old Mustang bar. Then they both turned around in their seats with guns pointed at me. As I stared down two barrels, the iron in my blood turned to lead in my ass.

"Maybe you should, run. Rabbit run."

My muscles felt frozen in place, while my mind and adrenaline raced.

Maybe getting murdered would be better than going to jail. They would have to shoot me in the car. I wasn't getting out.

After fifteen minutes or so of their little game, they turned the car around and took me to jail.

When I called my $10,000 attorney from jail, he explained that the charges were brought by Washoe County for an ounce of weed and couple grams of coke they had scraped from the scale and the bag, the coke originally came in the day they searched my house after my first arrest. I knew I should have thrown that bag in the garbage.

"I'll try to get them to run the charges concurrent with Lovelocks," he said. This meant instead of filling one county's sentence after the other, I could serve them at the same time.

After a night in county jail, I got released on my own recognizance.

Soon, I found that everyone I talked to when I was first bailed out had been wearing a microphone. They were all trying to rat me out. I wondered if it was because the cops knew I wasn't going to rat on anyone. So it seemed I was the scapegoat, the fall guy.

That's when I finally decided to heed my attorney's advice and not talk to anyone involved. Better late than never.

One Friday night, my friend Kenny and I sat nursing drinks at Balldini's nightclub. That's when he told me that a few days before Worm approached me, Worm had asked Stevie, a mutual friend of ours, to get him some coke. Luckily for Stevie, even though he tried, he couldn't. It was my fate to be the one who could.

"Man I can't believe you had to sell your truck," Ken said. He'd done such a kick-ass job on the paint helping me get it ready for Hot August Nights.

"You can't believe it; I've had that truck for three years now trying to get it done," I replied.

"After all that work I did on it," he said. "Eight coats of primer and ten coats of black, wet sanded in between each coat. You know that was a custom job."

"Shit that is one of the hottest paint jobs in town. I thank you kindly for all your work, Kenny."

Just then I saw a tall blond wearing a short black mini skirt with long slender legs that stretched all the way up to her shapely butt. I thought *if you had to have a wife, she would have to look like that.*

Her name was Betty. She was there with her sister Sharon. Kenny and I chatted them up. I soon discovered that, like me, Betty liked the outdoors, enjoying hiking, road trips to the mountains and ocean, or spending the day at Lake Tahoe. When she told me she drove a '76 280Z car, I thought about my beloved 280Z, confiscated in Lovelock for trafficking a controlled substance.

Figured, I finally met a girl that I liked and I had catastrophe hanging over my head. I didn't mention it. Maybe she'd like me and see that I was more than a bad mistake.

While the criminal justice system's wheels slowly turned, Betty and I spent a lot of time together over the next six months. We liked to go out to my family's ranch in Fallon to hunt or target practice. Or we'd travel to my sister's ranch at Pyramid Lake, where we would spend the days at the lake fishing or swimming and the evenings up at the ranch barbecuing and making margaritas. She wasn't much of a cook, so I was usually the chef. My sister Lucy ended up nicknaming her Betty Boufant, for the big blond hair do she always kept up.

One day while we were up hiking the natural springs up at my sister Lucy's ranch, I figured it had been long enough for Betty to know what kind of person I was. I figured I would throw the dice and tell her about the mistake I had made and the mess I was in. I knew time was winding down. I had to know just how much she liked me.

"Betty, there is something I have to tell you. Please understand why I have waited to tell you this."

"What, are you married?" she asked.

I laughed. "No, it's a little worse than that."

"Oh shit, what is it, Beef?"

"You see about six months ago I was set up and arrested for trafficking a half pound of cocaine."

"What?" she screeched, as she came to an abrupt stop on the trail. As she turned to look at me the sun was shinning in her eyes, I couldn't tell if she was squinting from the sun, or ready to cry. "Why didn't you tell me this sooner."

"I needed you to know me for who I am, not stereotype me for what happened."

She looked down, silent.

"I understand if you don't want anything to do with me. But you have to understand, I needed you to get to know me before I told you."

"I am no angel" she said. "My brother grows and sells weed in Oregon. I know people do these things. I'm just a little shell shocked."

My heart was about to break. I had to tell her how I felt.

"I understand if you want to break up. But I need to tell you, I have fallen in love with you."

Tears gathered in the corners of her eyes. My heart raced, waiting for her response.

"I love you too, Beef."

After another six months, we had a very small wedding at the Silver Dollar Queen in Virginia City, the same place my sister had gotten married a few years before, and where my parents were married in 1962. We moved into our own home in a nice quiet area of Reno. Perhaps getting married would prove to the judge I was changing for the better, improving my chances of minimizing my sentence. But more than that, I loved Betty. And I was amazed she was willing to stand by my side, no matter what.

My $10,000 attorney was busy telling me, "Don't worry about it, they don't want guys like you in prison. You're a first time offender. You'll more than likely get probation, or on the rare chance, if you do go to jail it will most likely be for three to six months in a summer camp having picnics on the lawn."

We believed him. We knew we could easily make it a year apart if I had to go away. We were prepared for the worst, yet hoped for the best.

Chapter 10: Night before Sentencing

Betty and I had been living together for several months when, one day, we were hanging out at my sister's ranch. We were sitting around the kitchen table talking, my sister's kids in the other room coloring with their colored markers. Betty disappeared for a moment.

When she returned she had a pink marker in her hand, playing like she was going to mark me with it.

"Try it, you won't like the repercussions," I said laughingly.

Lunging at me with the marker in hand like a sword, she drew a long pink stripe down my left shoulder and arm.

"Baby looks nice in pink," she taunted me.

I darted to my nieces' box of markers and grabbed the blue and black markers. I picked Betty up on my shoulder and spun her around a few times then gently lay her back on the floor. This would make her so dizzy she couldn't stand. Then I proceeded to make her one of my many masterpieces. Betty was a real Van Gogh by the time I had finished with her. A true piece of art, she sported multiple colors from the top of her blond head down to her toes.

For those few minutes, as was often the case with Betty's shenanigans, I was able to forget the mess of my life. If just for a few moments.

At several court appearances with my $10,000 attorney, Lovelock was not impressed with him. I think they threw the book at me for bringing a stranger to their neck of the woods. The judge and district attorney were very rude and harsh with him. Maybe I should have gone with one their good 'ol boys. I would have saved $7,500 and wouldn't have pissed off their backwoods judicial system.

The judge's right hand looked a lot like mine, like an awkward, unusable claw. It was difficult to see because he kept it well hidden with his robe. My attorney and I hoped this similarity might mean the judge would sympathize with me.

At one court date, my attorney left me alone to go talk to the D.A. to see if we could work out a deal.

Standing there in one corner of the courthouse with my family, I noticed how old and rustic the place was, its old checkerboard white and gray tiled floor. The old fashioned wood molding around the doors and ceilings was worn and dusty. I couldn't see anyone, but people's conversations and footsteps echoed throughout the building. But my parents, sister and her husband were silent. Surreal. I had no idea what to expect. What kind of deal might they ask me to accept? My stomach was in knots.

When my attorney came back into the room, he didn't smile. He didn't joke. He was all business.

"They want five to ten years out of you in prison if we plead guilty."

I couldn't believe what I was hearing. It was as though all the air was sucked out of me.

"What?" I screeched.

My family's faces were frozen in fear.

"The D.A. wants your ass. Between not playing ball with them and putting a hit out on his cop, he is bent on putting you away for a while. You should take the deal."

"What about the six months out at camp or a year like you said, picnics on the lawn, remember?"

"I think you should take the deal. If not, you could be sentenced to a lot more time. They want a decision from you today."

"If I don't give them a guilty plea today, they're going to come at us?"

"You could easily end up with twenty or more years," he said, his face somber. "I would take a moment and talk it over with your family and then give me a decision."

"Can we appeal their decision?" I asked.

"Yes, but that can take years. And it will cost a lot more money. The $10,000 only covers you up to the first court appearances and sentencing."

I had no more money. I had no more options. I had run out of rope. I knew I'd have to plead guilty. Today.

A few weeks later, with my sentencing date two days away, I had to go to San Francisco for a doctor's appointment. As Betty and I were finishing up dinner I thought it would be a good time to ask her.

"So have you decided whether you are coming to San Francisco with me on Wednesday?"

"No, I'm not going to go."

"What do you mean no? We can go the appointment and hang out at the pier and have lunch or dinner somewhere nice."

"I have work, I can't just take off."

"What in the hell? You know as well as I do this could be our last day together for one to five years."

"Oh, I don't really think it is going to be that bad."

Even though I was filled with rage, I merely stated, "Are you kidding me?"

No matter what I had to say, Betty was not going with me. She had made up her mind and that was final. I wondered what this was about. Was she pushing me away because I was headed to prison? Was she going to leave me after all?

So I called Bob, a friend since junior high and also our neighbor, to see if he'd come along. Short and thin with a full head of dark hair, Bob worked as a checker at the local super market.

"I'll buy us lunch, and maybe we could stop by the strip clubs I've been passing for the last couple years," I said, anger at my wife boiling under my skin. She'd really rather go to work than spend time with me on what might be our last day together for years?

"Sure, sounds good to me," he said.

After my doctor's appointment, we decided to explore the strip bars near Chinatown. Since it was afternoon, Bob and I were the only guys there, so we received all the attention.

With beautiful women in G-strings surrounding me and Jack Daniels warming my body, I was able to forget for moments at a time that tomorrow I was being sentenced in Lovelock. By 7 p.m., the girls were getting off work. They asked us if we would like to go get a bite to eat with them. They suggested a Chinese restaurant right around the corner. It was a very small and cluttered place with authentic and delicious food.

One of the girls suggested we get some alcohol, go down to the beach and make a bonfire. I had never partied on the beach of San Francisco and thought what a great adventure this would be.

It was now close to 10 p.m. It was a three and half hour drive back to Reno. The earliest we would make it back was 1:30 a.m. I figured we had enough time for another hour or two of fun. Down on the beach I was trying to repress the thoughts of Lovelock. And thoughts of my wife. I hadn't called her (this was before cell phones), and I was sure she was pissed. The more booze I drank, the more Bob and I laughed with these beautiful women, the fire flickering on our faces, the more I could forget what lay ahead of this sweet moment.

Sooner than I wanted to, I looked at my watch and realized it was 1 a.m., do or die time. We wouldn't make it back to Reno till 4:30 or 5 a.m. I had to be in Lovelock by 9 a.m.

A queasy feeling swept through me, fear of the unavoidable fear of the unknown.

"We have to get going," I said to Bob. We have one long ride ahead of us." As we started to gather our things, the girls protested.

"Don't leave so soon!"

"I wish I didn't have to," I said. Then I told them about my sentencing later that day. "I may be gone for a long time."

They gathered around me, "You're too nice of a guy for them to give you much time."

I laughed, "I agree. Thanks."

"Don't worry," they said. "It'll all work out."

When we got back to the car I'd driven Betty's 280Z I discovered the door was locked. I checked my pockets for the keys. They were nowhere to be found. I was starting to panic. If I missed this court date I would be considered on the run. A warrant would go out immediately for my arrest. What the hell did I do with the keys? I started to re-trace my steps down at the pier. I thought maybe I set them down somewhere. After twenty minutes of searching, I happened to look on a pole that held up the pier. Sitting on the top of the post were a set of keys.

Two car keys and a purple aluminum bottle opener on a key chain.

Betty's key chain had an aluminum bottle opener and two keys, but something just didn't look right. I couldn't figure out what it was.

The door opened after I aggressively turned the key. I had to shove the key in the ignition so hard I thought it might break. But the car started.

Bob and I hauled ass home. We hit the corners on I-80 coming into Verdi doing over 100 MPH. When the car got sideways and started to slide, I immediately lay off the gas and pulled the seat out of my ass.

I was finally home and Betty was, as expected, pissed. When I had just lain down in bed to regain my composure, she asked for her keys. I tossed them to her.

"These are not my keys!" she yelled.

What? These were the keys that had gotten us home. I got out of bed and went to the car. Pulling out the ashtray, I discovered her two keys with an aluminum bottle opener. Gold. Not purple. The wrong set of keys had gotten me home. It was if someone was watching over me that night.

Chapter 11: Sentencing

It was all I could do to drag myself up the steps to the court house.

My parents sat inside the old courthouse; along with my sister and her husband Len, waiting for me. Their eyes looked dark, like they too hadn't slept.

Nothing like being late to your own funeral.

Were they wondering if I was going to skip out? Believe me, I wanted to.

Worm and Butch stood there next to John David Black. Wearing suits, they were all cleaned up like never before, their smug smiles seeming to say *You should have become a rat like us!*

I wanted nothing to do with a rat deal, setting up other people to get out of my mistake. That's why the D.A. wanted my ass. I wasn't going to play ball.

Dread flooded through me. I had no more energy for this. I was running on empty. I had never before carried this much weight on my shoulders.

Finally, my attorney showed up, full of energy and ready to go, a big smile on his face. He obviously wasn't feeling the impending doom pervading the room.

"So let me get this right," said the judge, once we were all settled in our places. "Mr. Helm told you he had no problem getting you a half pound of cocaine to bring to Lovelock, Mr. Hole."

"Yes sir," said Worm. "He said he had done this before and knew right where to get what we needed." Worm was lying. I knew it. He knew it.

"Mr. Helm approached me," said Butch, "and asked if I knew where to get any cocaine. He also approached me to obtain anabolic steroids, Your Honor."

They said I initiated it all, including put the hit out on the cop.

"He actually approached you and asked if you would kill John David and or break his legs?" asked the judge.

"Yes sir," replied Butch.

"He was very angry that he had been arrested. He wanted Worm and John David to pay"

Every so often my attorney said, "I object." And every time the judge overruled it.

I sweat profusely, tangled in a surreal, nightmarish feeling. A big sentence was coming down; I just knew it. Soon I would be separated from my wife and family.

What was on the other side of those prison walls? Would it really be like the Tom Selleck movie, or worse? The unknown slithered over me like a python.

Voices began to sound like Charlie Brown's muffled teacher. My parents, my wife and my sister and her husband were all ghost white. How sorry I was for putting them through this.

Just hours before I'd been in San Francisco savoring fresh bean sprouts in the egg foo young. And the taste of the cold Sapporo. I probably wouldn't taste that again for years. *They won't throw the book at you. You are too nice a guy for something like that to happen.* What I wouldn't give to be back partying on the beach with the girls.

The Judge, looking like Jabba the Hut, cleared his throat, his damaged hand hidden in his robe. He was sitting up big and tall, his superiority looming over me.

"Well, Mr. Helm you seem to have a blatant disregard for the law," he preached. "You seem to be much more involved in illegal activities than you confess. I have never met anyone with such an antisocial personality."

I was the biggest outlaw that town had ever seen yet in my eyes I was a rookie. Was I really as bad as he was insinuating?

He slammed down his gavel. And what he said next chilled me to the bone.

"It is a good thing you decided to plead guilty, Mr. Helm. I was prepared to sentence you to twenty years in prison today, without batting an eye. However, since you decided to plead guilty, I am only going to sentence you to ten years in the Nevada State prison system. Although you will be eligible for parole within a third of that time."

My heart pounded through the wall of my chest like a wild stallion kicking through a barn door trying to escape. Nausea gripped my throat. Ten years? Was my fate that of my namesake, my Uncle Cliff Helm? In the 1920s he'd been an all-around world champion cowboy and then a bodyguard for a rich family in Nevada. He shot someone in self-defense, which landed him in the Nevada State Prison where he died from pneumonia. Was that my destiny, too?

Inconspicuously, I pulled some pills from my pocket: five Flexeril, five Halcion, and five Darvocet that I had tucked in there that morning. I thought if they did throw the book at me I would just go to sleep for a while or maybe forever. I swallowed them down with a couple gulps of water from the carafe sitting on our table in the courtroom. Perfect timing because not long after that I was cuffed, hands behind my back.

I glanced over and saw the devastated faces on my family. Their painful, sorrowful expressions will haunt me for all time.

Four days later I reluctantly woke up on a cell bunk in Pershing County jail, groggy and nauseated from all the medication. The cell was spinning.

Damn, I didn't take enough. I am still here.

Jim, the guy I had met last time I was here, loomed over me.

"Fuck, are you okay?"

"I'm not sure. Am I still here in jail?" I was trying to joke, but it fell flat. My energy was totally depleted.

"Yes, sorry to say, we figured you did not want to talk to or see anyone after we heard what they slammed you with. The cops were wondering when to wake you. At least they were cool enough to hear you snoring and not wake you. You probably need to eat something; it will make you feel a little better."

To my surprise, during my week in the luxurious Pershing County jail, the cops there were pretty cool with the inmates. If you needed to use the phone or ask a question they always obliged. They never really belittled you or gave you a hard time. It was like they understood that not everyone is perfect.

I knew it wouldn't always be like this. Other inmates told me some of the cops in prison were complete assholes. Some like to push your buttons and see how far they can test you.

I was also told the chow hall food was decent, but if you have cash on your books, you could buy stuff at the prison store or commissary like tuna, bread, sodas, coffee, ice cream, beans, tortillas and cheese. Also available for purchase would be hot pots and TVs. If you can get to know someone in the kitchen, then you will have access to fresh vegetables, eggs and milk. You have to learn to barter for what you want. You can also buy stuff with cigarettes; Camel non-filters are equal to cash. I was trying to get schooled. Any information would be good use for a fish stick like myself, a fish being someone who has never before done time.

The food in Lovelock jail was atrocious. Their most popular dish was this white flavorless gravy poured over tater tots with a mushy apple or withered orange for desert. The eggs looked to be powdered if you got any, and the food was delivered in Styrofoam containers. Lunches were usually a piece of bologna between two pieces of bread with a bag of regular chips, and dinner a hairy chicken leg and three Brussels sprouts.

The morning of my transfer, I was brought the breakfast of champions: soggy tater tots and some kind of egg concoction topped with the infamous flavorless white gravy. But it wasn't only disgust that turned me away from the food; I was so nervous and scared I could not eat.

They gaffled me up but not too tight, placing hand and ankle cuffs on me that were connected to a center chain.

"I don't think you're going anywhere are you?" the cop asked me.

"No sir, and thank you for not cutting off my circulation," I replied.

They politely walked me out the back metal door, and loaded me into the car.

"Watch your head," he said.

I scooted myself in and sat on the seat. I pressed the pins in my right thumb. What would happen to my hand in lockup? I hoped it wasn't a Gladiator school, where I'd have to fight the first day in.

An older man with long blond hair down to his butt was already loaded in the car next to me, laughing and smiling. I could tell by the way he was talking to the police officers he had a good rapport with them. He was acting like it was just another day in the park. Through their conversation, I got that his name was Doug. By the sounds of things the D.A. wanted Doug worse than he wanted me. And he wanted me pretty badly.

Doug didn't seem like a hard-ass or bad-ass but like a normal guy with a good sense of humor. I introduced myself and we chatted a bit, as though we weren't going where we were. At least I would know one person as I descended into this hellhole.

Chapter 12: Fish Tank

"Stand against the wall, toes first."

Still gaffled, Doug and I stood facing the wall while the guards prepared our paper work.

Soon, they walked us to a brick building in the back of the prison, behind yet another fence, with concertina wire coiled along the top. Dead Man's Alley, a twelve-foot space between two tall fences laced with razor wire, was wedged between the back building's yard and the main yard of the prison. That is where guards try to shoot those who attempt to escape. Dead man's alley wraps the whole prison yard.

Men in green uniforms, "pickle suits," loomed in towers with tinted windows. The ground was covered in decomposed granite, in which nothing likes to grow. No trees, no grass, no picnics on the lawn. Only white brick buildings with bars on the windows.

In the middle of the yard stood a cluster of pay phones without the privacy of the booths. The yard looked to be about a square mile, with the Sierra Mountains to the west, sand and sagebrush on the other three sides.

In the back building stood ten other fish inmates still in their street clothes, lined up with their toes to the wall.

A mountain of a man with a bad haircut, Moose yelled at us:

"Toes to the wall, don't talk! Don't look around! Keep your fucking mouths shut!" Probably in his early thirties, Moose had to be six-eight, if he was a foot, and weighed around 300 pounds.

A pickle suit un-cuffed us.

"Every one strip down!" Moose yelled.

We had no choice, of course. It was humiliating but no one said a word. Having only one usable hand I took longer than everyone else.

"Now bend over spread your cheeks and cough," ordered Moose.

"Run your fingers through your hair."

"Pull your ears out and forward."

"Open your mouth and show your gums."

He grasped my hands and looked thoroughly at them and then told me to bend over and cough again.

As we showered together in a large shower room, no one spoke. Dried off, we stood in a small room, arms out to our sides, our breath held, as they deloused us with a fine powder spray. Then they tossed us a nice bright orange jumpsuit even Jack LaLanne would have been embarrassed to wear.

Doug and I were tossed into the same eight by twelve-foot cell of white brick and concrete floor. A sardine can. It had a small window at one end and a bunk bed in the corner. At the opposite end was a stainless steel sink toilet combo like you see in the movies. We were numbered: 31344 was me and 31343 was Doug.

"You'll never forget that number," Doug told me.

He was right, I never have.

Right away I started to get a taste of prison life. It wasn't just the new fish that float through the fish tank. Anyone being transferred from one prison to another had to pass through. I had never seen so much ink; everyone was sleeved and displayed back, chest and headpieces. Tats everywhere. Uncertainty floated through the room like smoke. And so did the word *fuck*. *Motherfucking this* and *motherfucking that*.

A panicky feeling of claustrophobia sparked my veins. I was having trouble sitting in the small cell. How long could I stand being penned up? And it was only the first day.

Most of the pickle suits in the fish tank were hard asses. A short one with pockmarks on his face saw me looking at him.

"What the hell happened to your hands?" he asked.

Thinking he may be generally concerned I answered, "I lost the thumb in a drilling rig accident and my right hand in a fight."

"Pretty fucking stupid aren't you?" he spouted.

An immediate flush of anger and humiliation swept over me. Before I said something stupid and ended up on the wrong end of a nightstick, I looked away.

That evening we gathered in two-man lines and were escorted through the yard to the chow hall, after the rest of the yard was done eating.

"Don't look any one square in the eye," said Doug. "It is like you are disrespecting someone staring them down or calling them out."

In the main yard, most everyone wore blue denim; a few had regular clothes on. The fish in our orange jumpsuits stood out like angry pimples on a teenagers' face. Guys whistled and popped off at us.

"Hey fishy fishy, can't wait till you hit the yard."

"Better get to working out fish, we're going to bust your ass when you hit the yard."

The prisoners were of every color, size and shape. As we marched past the weight pile, we were eyeballed by some pretty intimidating guys.

Once in the chow hall, there are pickle suits everywhere. Some stand in bullet proof glass cages at the ends of the room, with shot guns out. Others yell at us to shut up, be quiet and stand in line.

The food looked better than at Lovelock, but there was no meat, just veggies, potatoes, carrots and celery, bread and pasta. I was happy to note an ice-cold serve yourself milk machine.

At my table sat a scary-looking guy: tall, lean, wiry; dark, thin hair; tatted sleeves, and a face full of scars.

"Hey man, I'm Ziggy," he said in gruff, low voice. "Just came back on a fucking parole violation, and now I have another fucked up five years to clean up."

Doug had told me in the cell to never ask what someone's crime was. So I kept my mouth shut.

"Are you going to eat that shit or what?" he asked. "This is pretty screaming food compared to county. Ever do time there, Clean Cut?"

"Nope, first time for me," I told him.

"I can sure as fuck tell you this man, if shit hits the fan in here, you dive under these metal tables to save your ass. Buckshot will be ricocheting everywhere!" He smiled.

Ziggy's white wife-beater shirt displayed the cobweb tattoos on his elbows, signifying he'd done serious time. He also had a teardrop tattoo, worn by someone one who'd done a hit in prison. Oh shit. I need this guy on my side.

Because prison tats are made out of cigarette ash (or sometimes smuggled-in ink), they are one color, usually blue, gray, or black. The tattoo guns are made from the little motors in a cassette player.

"Zig Zag Man," the image on rolling papers, was tattooed on Ziggy's upper right arm. Probably the origin of his nickname. Like many of the old timers, "White Pride" ran down his triceps. Ziggy kept mentioning his brother Big John who was already on the yard. I kept picturing Big John in Robin Hood. And indeed when I finally met him, he was huge. Three hundred pounds. I was soon to learn he'd already lost two hundred pounds!

Over time I would learn that Ziggy had been in and out of correctional facilities his whole life. You can tell when someone is hardened and institutionalized, the way they carry themselves, their proud and tough demeanor. Their grammar usually sucks, and most of their vocabulary is curse words. It was a good thing he liked me. He was tough. And until you go down you don't know the full definition of tough. You can feel it, sense it, and almost taste it. It's like a heavy thick cloud around a person; and you know in your gut, you do not want to piss this person off. I wondered, *how do I become that guy?*

Gilly, an older man close to Doug's age, also sat with us that first meal. At twenty-four, I was a baby compared to these men in their late thirties and forties. You knew Gilly was from San Bernardino, because he had it tattooed across his traps on his back. "Latin Pride" ran down his triceps. Like Ziggy he wore a white wife-beater and emanated the vibe of a lifer. But he had a thick, long dark ponytail.

"Hey Gilly, have you been to Folsom?" Doug asked.

"Fuck ya, man. That shit hole sucks; it's so decrepit and old. And a lot of old timers there. I was there in '83."

"Man I fucking hated Vacaville," Ziggy stated. "I was there in '83."

"Fucking try Chuckwalla," said Doug. "Talk about a fucking shit hole. The only good thing was that the warden would pitch a pound of weed over the fence once a month to keep the yard stoned and mellow."

How am I going to do this time?

Those words ran over and over through my mind as I lay on the one-inch thick mattress of my cot that first night. Yelling and talking echoed through the halls. I already missed my freedom. My family. My wife. I couldn't even be able to make a phone call or get mail until I got out of the fish tank. I almost felt like crying. But I knew that was the last thing I could do: shows weakness.

The next day after morning chow, Doug and I were out walking the little yard of the fish tank for our one-hour yard time. We saw a tree stump of a man, who had tied a towel to the bars of the cell performing isometrics. Then he dropped to the floor and did two dozen push-ups. About five feet eight, he was the width of two men but he wasn't fat; his bulk was pure muscle. His arms were so huge he looked like he could bench press a car.

Doug walked over to him and started talking to him. I followed like a puppy, eager to learn. By the way he talked, it was clear he was no stranger to being down.

"Hey Tiny what's going on?" Doug asked with a large smile on his face.

"Man just trying to get a fucking pump on. Kind of hard without an iron pile, brother."

"How much can you fucking bench?" Doug asked.

"Homes, I will rep 405 for 10 any day."

"I can believe that," Doug said. "Where you from, brother?"

"Man, I am from Southern Cali. Was up here on vacation and caught a fucking sex beef in Reno."

"Fuck, come to Nevada on vacation and leave on fucking probation," said Doug. Then he introduced himself and me.

"I'm Doug, this is Cliff."

"Baby Hog," the big guy replied.

The big guys who spend all day on the iron pile, driving iron, in the prison yard, the ones not with just big arms, but the huge guys who work out like a body builder, legs and all, they are called Hogs. Doug and I learned Baby Hog had been in and out of prison and youth camps all his life. An institutionalized life.

In the fish tank, we are not allowed to make phone calls or receive mail. No commissary privileges either. But a couple guys that were holed up with us because of overcrowding on the yard had hot pots and stingers. A stinger is a piece of metal connected to an electrical plug, used to heat water for coffee and soups. Considered contraband, a stinger could land you in lock-down. However, anyone that could not afford a hot pot risked it. I don't think there was a guy on the yard that didn't want hot coffee or soup.

I would soon be learning how to make every meal of the day, including my morning coffee, in a little Rival Hot Pot. Most popular was tuna ramen: a can of tuna in a Top Ramen soup. Everything was tuna this and tuna that. Tuna chili, tuna mac and cheese. We needed protein when working out, and tuna was the only way in prison. We very rarely got any kind of meat from the chow hall; instead they would potato, carrot and celery a guy to death. Anything we had for dinner one night was a soup for lunch the next day. Spaghetti for dinner meant spaghetti soup the next day. That was one reason I was so happy to see the self-serve milk machine; each cup of milk is seven grams of protein. We iron-drivers (weight-lifters) would try to guzzle at least six or seven cups of milk at the end of each meal. And I would soon be going through three to four cans of tuna a day along with the chow hall's food.

Top Ramen was as popular as cigarettes for bartering. Some of the prisoners had stores in their cells. Should you get cravings for a soda or sweets or popcorn or soup, you hooked up with those who had a store. Two candy bars or sodas cost you three back, meaning if you got two cans of soda or two candy bars, you paid them back what you got, plus one for the charge. Or if you wanted three of anything, you paid back five. I soon learned to appreciate such small gratuities as a candy bar or soda. Because some inmates had neither family nor money, they never would get to enjoy such luxuries.

Finally, after six weeks in the fish tank, it was time for Classification, which would determine if I'd be going to maximum or medium security prison or out to camp for picnics on the lawn. If you are lucky and within eighteen months of parole, you are eligible for camp: minimum security, no fences no gates. You either were on a fire crew or trash crew living outside the gates on the honor system. The fire crews would actually go up and fight the fires with the Hot Shots, a group of men that are the first ones to a fire. Often dropped by helicopters, it is very tough and dangerous work. Or you were on a crew that would be taken around to the parks and other public places to pick up litter and trash. Living outside the gates of the main yard obviously meant much more freedom.

If you were trouble you'd go to a maximum or medium security prison. All gang bangers and troublesome people went to Indian Springs, aka Gladiator School. They quickly learned to keep a magazine wrapped and taped around their midsection to protect themselves from getting shanked.

I was hearing from other inmates I'd probably be sent to camp since I was a first time offender. And I was excited to hear when I would be eligible for parole. Maybe eighteen months? I could do that. Hell, I had two months down already including my county jail time.

The classification board held their meetings in a spare room in one of the many housing units on the yard. A big room, with a chair for the prisoner being classified and a table for the three classification members to sit behind. When it was finally my turn, I walked in with a big smile on my face, trying to look as nice as possible and sat down. None smiled back.

"Michael Helm, 31344, you are charged with trafficking of a controlled substance level II. This comes with a minimum mandatory of at least five years. So you are eligible for parole in '95."

"What?" It wasn't easy to speak with the huge lump in my throat. "I was told by the judge I would be eligible for parole in a third of ten years. That's roughly three years, not five."

"The judge made a mistake and we will get five out of you before you are eligible for parole. You are not eligible for camp for three and half years. You have to be within eighteen months from parole eligibility."

So I would be twenty-nine years old before I even got to the parole board. Other inmates had been telling me that no one gets their first parole.

Oh, God. I would be stuck in here for six or seven years.

And no picnics on the lawn.

The board proceeded to ask me what I wanted to do: Kitchen or Prison Industries (PI), which meant working in the water bed manufacturing plant or one of the other revenue generating industries. They paid about thirty-two cents an hour, minus food and housing. It was a no-win situation, except perhaps for the long-timers holed up in here for ten or twenty years who had no one on the outside.

"Or you can do full time academic," said a chubby, unsmiling gray haired woman. "These programs will allow you to achieve good time and that comes off the back of your sentence, so in time it will shorten your stay. Not only that if you are full time work or academic, you have a chance to get into Unit Four. This is a two-man cell set up, and considering the rest of the yard is twelve men cells, there is quite a lot of motivation to get into the Unit Four."

I remembered my father's words: *If they send you to prison, you better take advantage of every class or program they have.* I knew this would be my only chance for rehabilitation.

"I would like to go to school full time if I may.'"

"That sounds like a good plan, Mr. Helm. We also recommend that since you have a drug offence that you attend N.A. as often as you can. This may help you receive your parole when you do go in front of the board."

"Hey Bitch, you tell him I am down, and when I get out I will fuck him up!"

I was standing at the phones on the yard, waiting to make my first call. The Crips and Bloods were hogging the lines. The dude in front of me was clearly a Blood: the crotch of his pants hung down to his knees, and a red bandanna hung out of his pocket.

"Yeah, that's right mother fucker," said a Crip with his blue do-rag on his head. "My fourth time down, I caught a quarter this time. Yeah, my brother and dad are out at Indian Springs. I can't wait to get there and help them out!" With their pants hanging so far down off their asses, I wondered how the hell they walked, ran or fought without falling down.

I tried my hardest not to make eye contact. But I was fascinated. I had never before seen a gang banger or better yet heard how proud they were to be down in prison: a notch on their warrior belt. The more times down, the higher up on the respect.

After fifteen minutes or so of this eye opening experience I called Betty for the first time in six weeks.

"Hello baby, how are you?" My voice starts to crackle. My eyes wanting to water up.

"Beef, how are you doing? I miss you so much." She started to cry.

"Are you sitting down?" I asked her.

"Why?"

"Fucking Dallas lied to us. I have a five year mandatory before I'm even eligible for a parole. I'm also hearing no one gets their first board. I'm probably going to be here for at least five or six years."

With a clenched gut and stinging eyes, I knew it would be much easier on both of us to not be married. There was no way I could wait for someone for five years. Why should I expect her to?

"I don't expect you to hang around," I said forcing out the words. "I want you to start divorce proceedings. There's no way in hell you can last or wait for five years."

"Oh, Beef, I love you so much. I will wait. Don't worry, I will be here when you get out."

I started to tear up again. I didn't think she would be willing to do this for me.

"Just do me a favor," I said. "If you want or need to go out on me, tell me first. Don't lie to me while I am in here."

I couldn't stand the thought of her with another man. That would just drive me crazy. I would rather her tell me before it happened so we could file for divorce.

"I can wait as long as it takes."

Next I called my $10,000 lawyer.

"Oh yeah," he said. "Trafficking Level II comes with a three-year mandatory. But they just changed the laws to a 5-year mandatory. But you were sentenced under the old law. I thought I told you this?"

"You never mentioned a fucking thing about a mandatory sentence," I said. "You kept telling us I would go straight to camp and be having picnics on the lawn, remember? No mention of a three-year or a five-year mandatory."

"No worries, the judge said you would be eligible for parole in a third of the ten-year sentence. The judge makes the sentence *not* the prison!"

"So what do we have to do?" I asked.

"Send me twenty-five hundred dollars and I can start with a sentence clarification hearing."

"Twenty-five hundred dollars to tell them what the judge ordered?" I asked.

"If you don't want the five years, this is what we need to do."

I'd find a way to get him the money. Still, helplessness flooded through me. *How in the hell was I going to program myself to spend years in prison?*

Chapter 13: Unit 3

After six weeks in the fish tank, I was transferred to a regular unit. These units, which run down either side of the three hallways, have dorms that hold ten to fourteen men. At the end of each hallway are four man dorms.

Unit Four was a privileged unit with only two men per cell. In prison this is equivalent to staying at the Hilton. Unit Four meant more privacy and less opportunity to screw up because you deal with one roommate rather than twelve. Full-time workers or full-time academics like myself could get into Unit Four. But I was missing one thing: a friend to bring me in. Unit Four was a lot like the unions; you had to be sponsored.

I was put into Unit Three. Doug, Gilly, Ziggy and Baby Hog all went to different units. So I was now in unfamiliar territory, I didn't know a soul. I was given a small yellow plastic tub to hold all of my personal belongings. As I walked in I could feel all the eyes on me, sizing me up. No one said a thing. They keep doing whatever it was they were doing; yet out of the corner of their eyes they watched my every move. Guys on their bunks, white on one, black on another, played cards and smoked Camel non-filters. Some guys slept, while others lay on their cots watching TV.

The little cots looked like something out of summer camp. Mine had a very thin and tiny mattress. Come to find out, I was lucky to get a mattress.

At the foot of each bed was your metal locker or your little yellow plastic tub containing your belongings secured with a padlock. When I left the fish tank I got to keep some of my clothes. It was pretty sad when I saw guys who had no one and nothing, wearing only a pair of old boxers and socks around the yard.

Only three feet separated beds. The walls were white brick, the floor gray concrete. Of course bars filled the windows.

At one end of each twelve-man unit was the shitter, four toilets with no seats. Behind a pony wall a few feet high were two shower heads and across from that three sinks attached to the walls. No stalls. No being shy there.

In the corner bunk, I saw this big blond guy, must have been six-two and two hundred and forty pounds. He looked as though he worked out often. I did a double take and saw it was Dan Mortion, from Fallon. We'd been friends at Fallon high school. In fact, he was my best friend's neighbor. We had known each other through wrestling, football and partying. Dan was always the biggest guy in school but the quietest with a very mellow demeanor. My nervousness immediately lifted when he saw me and recognized me.

"Big Dan, what the fuck?"

"Cliff, what the hell are you doing in here?"

"Fucking set up by a family member for a half pound of cocaine," I replied.

"No fucking way, really?"

I briefly ran down the story.

"You should have known better to take that amount out to Lovelock, brother." He laughed.

"I should have known better than to do a lot of things, Dan," I replied.

"Remember the times we used to eat acid or mushrooms and then go to football practice?"

"How could I forget? Talk about a trip trying to catch someone and seeing tracers!"

We went over old times and it felt good, like a brief moment of normalcy. As we continued talking he let me know his parole came through. He would be leaving in about three weeks. I was glad for him, but sad for me. Looked like I was going to have to find my way through this maze of prison etiquette on my own.

Lying on a bunk next to mine was an older gentleman, graying and probably is in his late forties. He was watching *Bonanza* on his little twelve-inch television: a scene where Hoss was riding to Nevada State Prison to see someone.

"Hey look at that," the man watching said.

They were showing the front of Old Max, the decrepit old maximum state prison that was actually about a mile away. *NSP* was engraved on an old rock wall out front of the prison, the place my uncle Cliff Helm died in the 1950s.

"What you here for?" he asked me.

He seemed to be a nice guy and not all caught up in the prison game.

"Trafficking, and yourself?"

I figured if he asked me my crime, I could ask him about his.

"Manslaughter," he said.

Maybe I shouldn't have asked.

He put out his hand, "Neil."

We shook hands, "Cliff."

Then he proceeded to tell me about his crime.

"I was partying with a neighbor, we were drinking and bullshitting, I must have said something to piss him off. The next thing I knew he went and got his gun and shot at me. So I got my gun and shot him dead. I figured it was self-defense. The jury didn't."

"Fuck, what kind of time did that get you?" I asked.

"Five years."

"What the fuck? I got more than that for trafficking a half pound of coke." A murder gets less time than a first-time drug offence?

"Why, what kind of time did you bring?" Neil asked.

"Ten years."

"Fuck they screwed you, didn't they? You must not have had an attorney."

"*Au contraire*, I had the most expensive attorney in the Reno area."

"Whatever happened to equal justice?"

I just looked at him and shook my head.

I was about two weeks in the unit when a tall skinny Crip, just a few cots down from me, was entertaining some of his dogs, three gang bangers laying on his cot. Not one of them over twenty-one years old. Their boom box playing hateful rap drowned out everyone else's radio or TV. And they were talking smack even louder. This wasn't the first time.

"Fucking A, I think chow will be screaming tonight, I am taking someone's shit tonight!"

"You ain't taking fucken' shit Nigga, it will be mine!"

"Fuck, I take what I want when I want!"

They looked around every time they shouted something, as if itching for a confrontation.

"Fucking monkeys," said Neil, just loud enough for me to hear.

"Always have to disrespect everyone around."

"You think they like the fucking music?" yelled a Crip.

"Fucking better," said my Crip neighbor. "I'm not turning it, better get used to it, I'm running things here."

They got up and walked out, leaving the radio cranked all the way up. Most of the inmates looked at them as they walked, shaking their heads in silence.

I didn't want trouble, I just wanted a little respect and to be able to think to myself or hear my own radio. As the Crip strutted back into the dorm to get something out of his locker, he was alone, his blue doo rag hanging from his pocket. He wore prison-issue blue jeans, the crotch down around his knees and a white wife-beater. He was taller than me yet very skinny and ripped. Having never really dealt with any blacks, especially a gang banger, I had no idea what to expect or what I was getting myself into. But I was undefeated wrestler and knew I could fight.

"Hey," I said, looking him in the eye, wanting him to know I was not afraid of him. "Think you could turn your radio down or off when you leave?

He just looked at me and laughed, his gold teeth shining in my face.

"Why don't you turn your shit down!" I said.

I felt heat and perspiration coming. My stomach tightened. I knew I was turning red.

"Don't fucking sweat me, fish," he said. Then his voice started to rise, "Fuck you mother fucking cracker. I'll fuck your white ass up! You better check yourself."

So here it was, I was having my first confrontation. Of course it had to be with a Crip gang-banger. I always have to go big!

"NO, fuck you, nigger."

"Let's take this shit to the shitter, fish!" he yelled back.

All the anger, hate and rage I had shoved down into my gut for the last year was about to erupt. As we headed to the shitter, I start to think, *What the fuck am I doing? I have no hands, nor shank jackass! He's a Crip. He's probably packing.*

Fear creeped into my bones, but I pushed it down. Fear causes hesitation. I knew I had to act, not react. I wondered, should I try to box this fuck or wrestle and take his ass down or my favorite move through the years of wrestling, body slam him on his head on to the pavement trying to smash it like a pumpkin. I was filling with more rage and fear than I have ever felt, adrenaline was pumping through my veins like never before. I figured I better box him. He probably had a shank. Better to not tie up with him, keep him at a distance.

When we hit the shitter we were both steaming hot like two raging bulls.

"Who the hell are you to tell me to turn down my shit?" he screamed.

"Show a little respect!" I yelled.

I didn't want to make the first move; I was waiting for him. Fear had already set in, clouding my judgment. We just stood there glaring at each other. Neither one of us wanted to push the panic button or make the first move. A few moments later we heard, *65 65 code*, meaning the guards were coming. I didn't want to roll up and go to the hole and apparently neither did he. While walking away, we glared each other down, knowing, this was not the end of it.

A couple of days later, Neil and I were sitting on our bunks. He was smoking a menthol and I was trying to. We were listening to the Hollies, "Long Cool Women in Black Dress."

"Stand up next to your locker!"

Neil and I looked around.

Bang, the doors smashed open as four guards rushed in from either end.

"Get up and stand by your cot!"

It was the goon squad, four to six guards who came to roll someone up, meaning they roll your belongings up and take you out of there. Usually to the hole. Or they take all of the pictures off the walls and search the space for contraband.

They gathered around my Crip buddy's cot, rummaging through his yellow box and everything he owned. I was thinking, *man I hope he doesn't think I ratted him out.* Altercations or not, you never rat. They started to tear his house down, go through all his stuff. We were all watching out the corners of our eyes. When they lifted his mattress, lo and behold, there lay a 14-inch shank. All blade with a small handle wrapped in tape. Was this shank meant for me? A cold shiver ran through my body.

Betty came to visit me every other weekend, appearing in hot little mini-skirts or tight spandex. All heads turned as she walks by. We would get something to drink and eat from the vending machines and then sit in a secluded spot on the old coffee-stained sofa or outside on the lawn. We would spend hours kissing.

"Helm, put some distance between you and her," the guard would order.

"Yes sir, sorry sir," I reluctantly replied.

"Oh Beef, I love you so much. It's so hard to not to get carried away," Betty said.

"I know sweetie. You think it's hard for you? Try walking back on the yard with a huge hard on."

"I don't care if you have to do the whole ten years, Beef. I will be here for you and wait for you."

"Thank you sweetie, that means a lot to me right now. I love you too."

"Beef, I want to buy a Jeep. They are so cool with the bikini top and all. What do you think?"

"I like them too. But don't get a four-cylinder or automatic. They are gutless and horrible on gas. If you get one, get a V-8 with a stick shift."

Time to leave always came too soon for us.

Sometimes my sister Lucy and my parents would come visit on Betty's off weeks. My father an old school veteran and cowboy gave me a hard time about my long hair. I'd let it grow down to my butt. One time I had my hair pulled back tight in a ponytail.

"Finally I see you cut your hair like a man," my father said.

I just laughed and turned around to show him my ponytail.

"Nope, just pulled it back for boxing,"

"You need to cut that shit off; you look like a girl."

"I will for my parole hearing." I told him.

"Hey Dad, ease up," said my sister.

We would talk about everything and nothing, eating microwave popcorn and drinking sodas. I envied the mundane details of their free lives.

At the end of visits, it was like leaving a dream world and then facing cruel reality. Many prisoners tell their families to not come to visit. It's just too painful. Family and friends are a reminder of the life you are no longer a part of. It's best when in prison to forget about the outside and just do your time. But I couldn't do it. I cared too much about my family.

In fact, it was in visiting where I met a sister for the first time, a sister I never knew I had. My mother had written the family a letter telling us that before she had married my father, she'd been married to his stepbrother Wayne. Together, they had three children. Two I grew up with as sisters, but one, Donna, she'd given up for adoption right after birth, without anyone knowing, because her marriage to Wayne was ending. Soon after, she married my dad. And a few years later, when I was about six years old, Uncle Wayne, an alcoholic, died from sclerosis of the liver.

While I was in prison, Donna found and contacted my mother. My sisters and I were shocked to learn we had another sister. Donna was going to be coming from Clovis, New Mexico to meet my parents and family. When they told me she wanted to come visit me, I was very hesitant. I didn't want to meet my sister for the first time behind prison walls. But my family persuaded me.

When I entered the visiting room, I saw a woman with dark hair who looked like a younger version of my mother. As I approached her from across the room, she gave me a big smile. She must have seen a picture of me to be able to have recognized me. She gave me a big hug.

"So you're my brother?"

"Yes, sorry we have to meet like this," I said, humiliated.

"Don't worry about it," she said. "I've seen worse."

"Good, because I haven't."

"Everyone makes mistakes; it is what you do about it that defines the person."

Dr. Brown contacted the prison and told them he needed to see me. He needed to remove the pins in my right hand and thumb before they got infected. The prison decided to take me to Reno to my old doctor. Charles McCuskey, who would do the surgery at Washoe Medical. I had not seen Dr. McCuskey, who knew my family and me for years, since I had been arrested.

There I was wearing an orange jumpsuit, cuffed to the bed, when he walked in.

"Hello, Michael how are you doing these days?" he asked with concern.

"Not too good doctor, as you can see."

The last time I had talked to him, Dr. McCuskey was bending over backwards to do whatever he needed to save my right hand so I could still live a normal decent life. Now here I was cuffed to a bed, in an orange jumpsuit. I could barely look him in the eye.

"Michael it will be a quick operation. I'm just going to remove the pins from your thumb. You should be up and running in no time, if they allow that."

"Thank you, sir. I greatly appreciate it." I replied, as I swallowed any pride I had left.

Without a smile or a grimace, he just looked away, got up and walked out of the room. I could tell by the way he acted he was very disappointed in me. Then the nurse came by to insert the IV and see how I was doing.

"How goes it, Michael?" she asked.

"Oh it goes. I'm pretty embarrassed Dr. McCuskey saw me like this. He has performed many surgeries on me since I was a kid. And now I have to face him like this."

"Don't let it bother you or get you down," she said. "We all have troubles growing up. I have seen worse and think you will do just fine when it is all over." Her words echoed those of my sister. They were two angels in my life.

After all the surgeries and having the casts on my right hand and arm for so long my muscles had atrophied. My whole arm was only as big around as my wrist. I knew I had to fight the pain and any handicap to get back in shape. The first time after the surgery that I tried to curl a two-and-a half-pound dumbbell with my right arm, it felt like someone was trying to snap my arm in half. I had no grasping ability with the right hand so I had to learn to tie all the weights to my hand for any pulling movements. And for pushing movements, I had to create some kind of padding for the palm of my right hand because it was just bone under the skin. I was in extreme pain just trying to bench press the weight of the bar. I could barely bench press 135 pounds.

I got notice I had been accepted for an appointment to the prison infirmary to see a Dr. Ghedney, whom, I was amazed to see, was a blond bombshell sitting behind a big gray metal desk. When she stood up to shake my hand, she was taller than I and built like a model.

"Hello. I am Dr. Ghedney, how are you?" She asked. "Why don't you have yourself a seat, Mr. Helm?"

"Thank you, ma'am." I replied, wondering how and why such a beautiful woman would want to work in a prison.

"What can I do for you, Mr. Helm?"

I explained that I wanted nylon straps to wrap around my wrist and barbell to help me grip and pull, in order to rehabilitate my arm.

"I've seen those before at the gym," she said. "I think I can accommodate you with those."

"As you can see I have no padding under my skin between the bone and skin on the palm, I could use some kind of lifting gloves that will provide me with a little padding too."

"No problem, Michael. I like the that you have the motivation to do this, and not just sit around and let your muscles atrophy. If there is anything you ever need, just ask."

I spent every spare moment reading body building and lifting rags. I rapidly began to bulk up. Soon I became the guy on the yard people came to with questions about nutrition and working out.

Doug, Gilly, Ziggy and I took pictures of ourselves to monitor the changes. Most days I'd bullshit with the hogs on the yard. Baby Hog and I always ribbed each other and gave each other shit. I also met guys like Woody, a huge guy, 6 foot 4 inches, 240 pounds, who sported a total back piece tattoo of two Harleys coming out of a Pan Head and Shovel Head motor, which also incorporated a couple topless ladies. He always had a smile on his face and seemed to be of good nature. Then there was

Rock. He was my height, only a little leaner, sporting dark hair and a goatee; he always sported the KD sunglasses, black plastic frames and tiny blue, red green, or black lenses, the kind old bikers and old school inmates wear. He and Woody had been down for over ten years. They'd come over from maximum security for good behavior.

I also met a cool cat named Bobby Bolin, one of the best tattoo artists on the yard. He was sleeved up with single color tats and always wore the KD style sunglasses. Bobby was laid-back and usually stoned, doing easy time, tattooing the days away. He, too, had been through max and was now here on this yard for good behavior. He was the one who taught me how to get stoned in prison. We would have a look out, while Bobby would roll the tiniest joint I had ever seen, the size of a toothpick. He knew the cops' schedule like clockwork. When it was time, we would sit on his cot. He'd light the tiny joint and take a hit and pass it. We held it in as long as possible then exhaled into a tightly wrapped towel that would absorb the smoke and conceal the aroma.

After I got stoned with him a few times, I started to think *if I get caught doing this, I will never get out of here.* And I could face being rolled up and shipped to Indian Springs. That was enough of a deterrent, to get me to quit.

I started to do haircuts for a fee of six packs of Camel non-filters. I could generate smokes quickly by cutting hair. Smokes were like cash in prison; most everything was bought and paid for with cigarettes.

The first few cuts I did in prison, I thought, *I better not mess this one up or I could end up dead or maimed.* It was pretty nerve racking cutting an ax murder's hair for the first time, especially when he liked a flattop with a fade.

For every haircut, I had to give two packs to the Cuban, Vic, for the use of his shears. An older gruff man with little sense of humor, Vic had slicked-back dark hair and he always wore a white wife-beater.

There was no bullshit when dealing with Vic. It was obvious he had no patience for fish; you better check yourself well when doing business with him.

I'd been down about twelve months when I decided I wanted a tattoo.

Bobby was sitting on his bunk drawing out new tattoos for other inmates.

"What's up, Homes?" Bobby said.

"Hey man, what will you charge me to sling some ink?" I asked.

"For you my son, eight packs of Camel non-filters. I usually charge twelve. You also have to pay for the lookout which will be two more packs."

"Ten packs total?" I asked.

"Well, what exactly do you want done?" He asked.

"My old roommate had a Snoopy on his calf, and he was flipping you off, I kind of thought that was cool. Only I want the Tasmanian Devil flipping you off, with a ball and chain around his ankle."

"Ten packs total then for that, brother." Bobby stated.

"That includes look out?"

"Yes, I will start drawing it up as soon as you give me four packs to start."

When the day came, a guy sat in the hallway, keeping watch for guards. He'd yell "SIX-FIVE" if anyone came. It's illegal to get a tattoo in prison; getting caught meant landing in the hole or Indian Springs. My nerves were a wreck.

As soon as Bobby hit me with the needle, *OUCH!* I felt it but couldn't say it. What prisoner wants to come off as a pussy? I just laid there for four hours off and on, scrambling up to my bunk to act like I was reading when we heard "SIX-FIVE!" After the guard walked by giving us the eye, we would get at it again. When finally finished, Bobby smothered it in Vaseline and told me to wear pants for two weeks.

"Just keep it covered man."

By that time, I was starting to get some size on me. Bobby wanted to sleeve me up with tattoos.

"Man, you are getting big; you would be looking fucking BAD with sleeves," he'd say.

"Man I wish I could, you are a great fucking artist, but I'm planning on going to school for x-ray or ultrasound one day when I get out of here. I don't want to be stereotyped, especially if I ever get pulled over by the police. I don't want the hassle."

But you don't go into the joint or into the service without getting at least one tattoo to remember it by.

Looking back at my time spent in prison, it didn't seem so bad or so long. However, when looking ahead at the time left, it seemed to stretch on and on. Sometimes it felt like it would never come to an end.

Doug and Gilly, who worked in the kitchen, said many of the boxes of food received were labeled, "*not for human consumption.*" I always wondered if they were pulling our legs. They would often bring us jalapeño peppers, fresh garlic, and cheese or eggs, out of the kitchen for a cheap price. Foods that can be eaten quickly or shoved into a shirt pocket. These types of foods were not available in the store.

Eating two to three dozen eggs and drinking twenty cups of milk a day, Doug and Gilly grew faster than the rest of us. To stay anabolic and build muscle you want about two grams of protein per pound of body weight a day. That can add up. I needed 500 grams a day.

After breakfast I would go out to the iron pile where I would meet up with Doug, Gilly and or Ziggy to lift for about three hours. At the iron pile, we'd size everyone up. There were actually two iron piles, one in the gym, which was very loud and cramped and smelled of old gym socks. Basketball courts and old wooden bleachers ran down the sides of the courts inside the gym. The Blacks and Heavies team would always take the gym, to avoid the heat and or cold of the weight pile outside. Heavy was an African American standing maybe five-five, and weighing about three hundred pounds. Yet he was one of the strongest blacks on the yard. He always had his clique around him and they always had an attitude. He could bench four hundred pounds but when he went to do squats, he would load the bar with four to five hundred pounds and then barely bend his knees. He was so short, I think, he thought he was going all the way down to the bucket, which means doing full squats as if you are sitting down onto a bucket, then standing back up. We would always watch and snicker and yell smack to him about it. This would piss off him and his dogs. The gym rats would come outside and haul away as many of the weights and dumb bells as they could back into the gym. Then in return we would have to go back in and haul them out again. It was a viscous never ending-cycle.

Most Mexicans and us whites worked out outside under the guard tower. It was all about dedication there. You did not let anything stop you from your program.

On hot summer days if you did not pour water on the weights before you grabbed them the hot iron would burn you. If you put a bar with 400 pounds on your back for squats it would burn a mark across your traps. Because I liked to do front squats, I had burns and bruises on my sternum and deltoids from doing 400 pounds. No padding on any of the equipment made us tough.

In frigid winter, when it would drop to minus seven degrees or lower, we would layer on five or six shirts and then a sweatshirt. One night it snowed three feet; we had to find, then dig out the weights and benches, the snow was so deep. There were no collars to hold the weights on the bars. So we had to improvise. We would sprinkle mud and sand on the end of the bars to keep the weights from slipping off. We would have to shovel out the benches and make routes around the iron pile through the snow. Imagine squatting 400 pounds on ice. The steam rose from our shoulders and ice developed on our backs. Our eyebrows and beards would be iced over.

After working out I went back to the cell for lock-down and a standing head count. Then off to lunch, after which I would go to take my high school classes. They were held in the small white brick educational building. The teacher Mr. B. was quite a character. An old man in his later seventies, he had white hair and was full of spunk. As I sat in class, I wished I had taken advantage of my high school and scholarships when I had the chance.

Mr. B always had the coffee pot on, a good thing since most the time it was all I could do to stay awake through class. Full of food from lunch and tired from my workouts, my eyes threatened to close as I sat in the comfortable climate-controlled room.

One day I was sitting in my usual position: feet up on the table and leaning back in my chair, hands behind my head with fingers laced together, testing how far I could lean back before almost eating it. Mr. B started lecturing on how the government was doing something ridiculous.

"This is how stupid our government has become," he said, his cloud of white hair lit up under the florescent lights. "It's rewarding agencies and bureaucracies for pure recklessness and wastefulness."

"How is that? I asked.

"The government is on a self-destructive mission right now, rewarding agencies and bureaucracies with a bigger budget every year as long as they use up the previous year's monies and supplies, even if they don't need it and can't use it up wisely. Instead of the government rewarding stringent budgets and cost saving policies, it is busy throwing money down the toilet. If agencies use their entire budget, they receive a budget increase every year. People are locking up and throwing away supplies and money to assure they will receive even more the next year."

I wondered how the hell this could continue without breaking the bank. It couldn't and didn't; California went bankrupt. Mr. B actually sparked my interests in political science. He also got me thinking about the gold standard when he told us that gold would once again become very valuable because the United States was printing money without the backing of gold to ensure its value. Later I purchased two ounces of gold for $385 an ounce. If I would have held on to it long enough I would have seen great returns, as gold did skyrocket to the price of almost $2,000 an ounce in recent years. However, I sold when the price was hitting $500 an ounce. No one could imagine that it would hit the prices that it did, except Mr. B.

Chapter 14: Unit 4

All night I listened to every sound, every little crack, click or snore. When I finally fell asleep, I'd sometimes be shaken awake by a guard. During the multiple night head counts, the guards woke you if they couldn't see your head or feet. In addition to those intrusions it simply was not possible to be comfortable on a one-inch-thick mattress lying on a metal shelf. There were certainly no select comfort settings. I craved my bed back home, my pillow, how I used to fall asleep in minutes and sleep like a rock. I could nap whenever I wanted, wake from a dream, get up, do something and go back to the dream. It had been more than a year since I slept thoroughly. I wondered if I would ever be that comfortable again.

Meanwhile, prison as hard as it was, opened my eyes. I first heard about the "Moes" from Doug and Gilly during our meals while in the fish tank.

A Moe had an entirely different prison life.

One Moe, Marty, had a mane of long blond hair that bunched up like a bad perm. She usually wore shorty shorts or skirts. When wearing jeans, she paired them with a pink-half top sweater.

When Marty didn't shave she looked pretty grim. I wondered how a guy could possibly be attracted to her; the guys that had been down at least ten years seemed to go in that direction. A Moe catered to her man's every need. She'd be by his side in chow and everywhere on the yard. She'd carry his radio, jacket, or laundry so his hands were free. Some Moes had sex change surgery, but most didn't. Sometimes we would have six or seven Moes on a two thousand man yard. White ones, black ones and Asian.

Then there was Cindy. She was little and wore her mousy brown hair in pigtails, and her face was always made up, eye shadow included. She was nice to me. She would always smile to me and say hello or compliment me on my build, my smile or my clothing. However, I did not pitch or catch. We figured it did not matter if you were pitching or catching, you were gay! Sure, you could argue it's a situational behavior due to being locked up. However, I did not look at it that way. I knew some guys that were playing around in there, yet they would *not* want it known on the outside. Probably ninety-nine percent of them wouldn't want anyone to know what they were doing.

One of my cellies, Rock was one of these guys. He had a Moe. Sometimes I would walk in and they would be sitting together, her rubbing his legs or shoulders and or cleaning his cell. She'd make him stuff to eat and do his laundry, keeping his cooler full of ice and catering to his every want and need. She always talked to him in a very gentle and feminine voice. Luckily I never walked in on them doing their *other* thing. That wasn't something I wanted to see or hear.

Some of the guards made our lives hell. Others eased our pain. Two brothers, the Kennedys, were at opposite ends of the spectrum. The younger one had short man's disease; he used his power position to compensate for his insecurities. The older brother, though, was a sergeant, and very cool. When our bi-annual packages came in, if Sergeant

Kennedy wasn't at receiving, we'd come back when he was. He ignored things that most guards would bust our balls about. If the clothing in a package we received wasn't quite regulation colors or something small like that, he didn't care, unlike his brother who would hassle you and make you send it back.

We were allowed two twenty-five pound packages sent in each year for Christmas and birthdays. The first year, my family sent me a blue bedspread and pillow, jeans and lots of blue sweats, shorts and tanks tops. For the remainder of my time the packages were the same. And everyone on the yard loved me! Woody still rants about how cool it was to be my cellie when I got my packages. I would call home and request twenty-five pounds of oatmeal raisin cookies and twenty-five pounds of beef jerky. My birthday is Christmas Eve, so I'd get 50 pounds at a time each year. High in protein, jerky was a commodity on the yard. Some of those guys had not tasted jerky or cookies like these in more than ten years.

After the first year I noticed Betty's visits were becoming less regular. She had decided she wanted to move in with my cousin's ex-husband, Spot. Supposedly this was to save money on rent. He had purchased my aunt and uncle's old house, which was rather large, with extra bedrooms and bathrooms.

I felt uncomfortable about this but didn't say anything. And even if I did oppose it, how could I stop it? I thought she would behave herself and she could save some money. She and Spot hung out with my sister and her husband, the four of them going to Las Vegas and other cool places. Like two couples. I asked my sister if she thought Betty and Spot were messing around. She assured me they weren't. My intuition, however, told me Spot was Sancho. Sancho is the guy doing your wife while you are down.

One day I was talking my cousin Lori, Spot's ex-wife, on the phone. She told me that her five-year old daughter asked her, *Why was daddy kissing Auntie Betty?*

I was shot in the gut with massive pains and my head started to hurt. But I'd known it all along. Finally, I got Betty on the phone. She had been avoiding my calls and my visits.

"You fucking cunt!" I yelled. "How could you do this to me? "I told you, to tell me if you wanted out of the marriage before you have an affair, and you promised me you would."

"I'm so sorry," she said. "It just happened,"

Hearing it in her own words, the reality smacked me in the face. "I knew this was going to happen if you moved in with him!" I screamed.

"I didn't think it would happen," she said, her voice wobbling. "But I think I love him."

"You need to start a divorce and start sending me the paper work to sign. This is over! And you can tell Spot when I get out, I am going to have his head!"

For days on end, I was filled with anger and frustration. I could not eat or sleep. On the outside you can go have a drink and blow off steam, or go hang out with your friends or family for support and sympathy. Maybe go out and see someone else, if you wanted too. Take a drive, go for a ride, or hike in nature somewhere serene and get your thoughts together. You have options to help deal with the pain and frustration. However, in prison you have to handle your emotions and feelings privately. You don't want anyone to know what is going on personally. You can't show weakness or sorrow. Sure, you can go drive iron or go run a few miles, not to mention go get in a fight. However, you are locked up with assholes and guards that are only pushing your buttons. Whatever you do might not help and probably would work against you.

A year and half down now, I was getting big and strong. One day I was lying on my bunk watching live coverage on the local news of a high-speed chase between the cops and an ex-felon. He was hauling ass, wrecking into cars and smashing his way down the avenues. I was thinking, *you motherfucker, it's people like you that give us a bad rap, making it nearly impossible to get a parole.* Turns out, he was friends with old-timers like Woody and Rock and a few others.

His name was Goat. And lucky for me: when he was brought into the yard after the fiasco broadcast on TV, with help from some old timers, he and I were pulled into Unit Four. Unit Four was like being downtown, no more fools in your room. You could just shut the door and everyone else out: a two-man cell with a stainless sink-toilet combo. We kept it spotless like most guys. Most guys I know who did time are very clean. OCD clean. Perhaps it had something to do with having to share a very small place.

Goat introduced me to earplugs. The two-man cell was so much quieter and now with earplugs I could actually sleep. The sense of knowing I was in a little safer place allowed me to relax.

Soon, though, Goat got rolled up for contraband and sent to the hole for a few weeks. That now made it impossible for him to get back into Unit Four. Woody became my cellie. Woody was cool, old school, and he treated me with respect.

One-day Rock and I were alone in my cell; I didn't know him as well as I thought. We started sparring. I thought we were just goofing off, throwing jabs and kicks at each other as I had done this with friends on the outside. The next thing I knew, Rock threw four or five series of punches. The look in his eye…I'd never seen it before. Almost like a rabid dog. I sensed now that he was not screwing around. I was shaken, unsure what to do. I realized if I took it to the next level, I could get shanked. I thought I knew this guy, but then it struck me: *You never really know anyone in prison.* I didn't want to throw the next punch or kick. I figured I would leave that to Rock. We stood there in a stare down, like two boxing statues. Suddenly, Woody walked in and told Rock to cool off and get out of the cell.

"Never take Rock too far," said Woody, after Rock had split. "He's a third degree black belt. He may just fuck you up for fun. He just likes to put everyone in check."

Going to college classes meant walking under the gun in the evenings to the education building, dropped off and locked in. It took me the first year to finish my high school courses to get my diploma. Sporting a blue graduation cap and hair down to my butt, I had the picture to prove it. There wasn't a ceremony, only cookies, punch and a photo shoot. Next goal: college.

Out of 2,000 guys on the yard, only a handful took advantage of college courses. I paid for most my college classes with a Pell grant. Dr. Ghedny taught all the anatomy and biology courses, and Dr. Kulik was the psychology instructor. In her sixties, Dr. Kulik had a heavy German accent and tightly curled auburn hair. Sometimes when a student answered questions, she would tilt her head back and give him a penetrating stare with her big brown eyes. When she did that, you didn't know if you were dead right or dead wrong; you had to pause for a moment to detect her next emotion.

After a few semesters she became my favorite teacher. When I explained to her that I was going through marriage difficulties, she told me that when her husband died she threw herself completely into her studies, striving to get through school to help her get over the heart ache. She suggested I do the same. The way she took time with us to make sure we were clear on a topic before moving on, made me realize she really cared. To ease our test anxieties, she would bring suckers and hard candies to class. This was a treat that we all appreciated very much. Her praise and positive reinforcement made me feel good about my efforts and myself.

By majoring in Psychology, I thought I would like to help kids in trouble or those with disabilities. I was seeing a change for the better in myself and it felt good. I was beginning to understand the human psyche and actually taking the responsibilities for my own actions. By not blaming others for my foolish mistakes, I started to understand that my troubles were my doing. As hard as it was to accept the blame, it was also empowering. That meant I had control over my life. If I had the power to make things go wrong, I had the power to make them go right. Perhaps I could help someone young before they made the mistakes I did.

I was also starting to get into excellent shape and could bench 315 pounds even with my handicapped hands. It was about this time I met Burt Hoffur through the schooling and working out. Burt, a tall, lean dude a blond with a rat tail he always kept braided, seemed to be very normal, someone I could relate to, with a calm demeanor and attitude. And he was from Carson City, near my hometown. One day on the weight pile, Burt told me his offence. He had gotten into a confrontation one day and beat a guy with a baseball bat. I can't remember what caused the fight, but I do remember him telling me he beat the guy within an inch of his life. He ended up with a ten-year sentence and had done almost five of it. God, I hoped I would not have to do five on my ten. Our conversation lead me to telling him about Tana, who'd been living in Carson City when she was murdered. I was telling him the story of how she was killed by her boyfriend right after I got busted.

"I knew that guy Beef, I actually played softball with him."

"Really?" My adrenaline spiked through the roof. I started to breathe hard and get anxious. I wanted his blood.

"He was a cocky asshole." Burt replied. "Never knew Tana, but I had heard what happened. I'm sorry."

"I kind of wish he hadn't killed himself, Burt. I would have liked the honor of doing it for her."

"Oh it would have been a good fight between the two of you, Beef," Burt said. "It's probably a good thing he did it for you. You would be in for life if you did that, you know."

"I know, but you know Burt, sometimes the consequences do not matter when you are seeing red."

We never talked about it again. No matter how much I rehabilitated, how much psychology I learned, there were some things that would still set my anger and revengeful emotions on fire. Just the *thought* of seeing the man who had murdered my first love in cold blood, raged war and havoc on my cognitive ability to stay calm. *God, would I ever be able to stop getting in trouble?*

Woody had introduced me to JW, his old cellie from max. An ex-hit man from Vegas, JW was also a professional boxer. I asked JW if he would train me to box. Maybe boxing could be something I could share with kids to help them get strong and take out their frustrations in a positive way. I also thought boxing, combined with my college courses, would help me pass the time. My divorce was almost complete. I was no longer feeling so bad about it. Her loss, I figured. I would come out a better person, with or without her.

JW was huge. He was in his forties and could out run me any day of the week. His head was as big as a buffalo's and hard as a rock. In fact, anywhere you hit this guy it hurt your hand. His hands were twice the size of mine. Even his slight jabs were bone crushing. I could not imagine being hit in the face by this guy without gloves. Dark brown and hair and light-complected for a Native American, he always had a smile on his face and great attitude. Like Woody, he had been down a very long time.

One day when we were getting a breather in after a three-mile run, he told me, "I used to run through the Vegas desert in combat boots to stay in shape when I was boxing."

"You had to be in great shape, man," I replied.

He said he would wear gloves with powdered lead sewn into the knuckles for hits. This would crush the bones.

He made Mike Campbell, a friend of mine who was also in Unit Four and me, walk the line for a month before we were allowed to hit the bag. Up and down the lines on the asphalt of the basketball courts, we'd walk and throw punches in the air for hours a day. Push, step, slide. Push, step, slide. You push off the rear foot and step with the front foot as you throw the punch and slide your back foot up, so you are back in stance. Or reverse for backing up and throwing. Push, step, slide. If you land your punch at the exact same time you land your step, then you have your hips into it. Nothing is stopping you. You can't feel the pressure if done correctly. I would soon learn to land a jab that would put a lot of guys down.

JW taught us body punches for headhunters: fighters that just try to hit you in the head. That means their bodies are usually wide open. If you land a left to their liver, it will put them in shock, game over.

I had a smiley face permanently marked on the heavy bag hanging on the basketball hoop. His name was Spot on one side and Worm on the other.

One day while visiting with my sister Lucy, I was coming back from the vending machines with bag of popcorn and a few snacks not available on the yard. As I was sitting down on the gray coffee-stained couch, Lucy asked, "Where's Hatch?" simultaneously putting her hand up to her forehead like a hatchet.

I yanked her hand down and hissed, "Don't let him see you do that!"

Hatch, was a good friend of mine from Unit Four. He did college courses and was married to a psychologist, who often came to prison for church; that's was how they met. She had previously been cleared to be an instructor for college courses and a counselor. She started to come and help with the church services, also. Hatch had been down eighteen years and worked his way to the medium security yard. Quite a feat for a hatchet murderer.

He and his road dog, Chuck, worked out religiously like anyone else trying to program their time. Hatch was built like a bullet. One day he decided to tell me his story. He was dating a woman who had an old man. They made a plan: she would have sex with her old man on the living room floor and Hatch would be hiding behind the couch with an ax. Hatch would hit him in the head with the ax. But in a deal she turned state's evidence against him for less time. She got the deal because she hadn't actually done the killing. I thought he had to be one cold blooded dude to do something like this. Balls of steel. Hatchet had been to many a parole hearing but had never gotten a yes.

One day Hatch asked me if I believed in Christ. I said yes I did; I had been raised Catholic. He proceeded to tell me of an annual prison event during Easter. At this event they'd baptize volunteers in the name of Christ. He explained this was the only way to be accepted by God into heaven as a Christian. And that as a Christian we studied the Bible, not a religion as in Catholicism or Mormonism and other religions. Maybe being baptized would be good for me. Maybe I could be forgiven for all the bad I had done throughout my life. I'd rather be taken into heaven than banished to hell, and given my track record; I was on the fast track to the inferno. It couldn't hurt to better myself along with my relationship with God.

There I sat in the gymnasium, with crooks, ax murderers, and others who'd committed heinous crimes. We gathered together, looking for forgiveness from a higher entity than mankind. A very emotional event for me, it was several eight-hour days of learning and studying the Bible. The last day of the event, on the day of my baptism, Hatch called my name:

"Cliff Helm, please come forward."

As I stood up and proceeded to the podium and trough of ice

cold water, a large lump developed in the back of my throat. My heart started to race, and I was sweating profusely. As my eyes filled with tears, I fought back an uncontrollable urge to cry. *Do not cry. Do not cry. Don't let your guard down in front of these men.* Yet something much more powerful than myself was tugging at the tears. I knew Hatch could see what was happening to me. He actually gave me a hug.

"Let go and let it happen," he said.

The tears poured down my face. I couldn't believe I was crying in front of everyone. But there was something softening in me, something releasing. It was unlike anything I'd felt before.

"Do you, Cliff Helm, take Jesus Christ as your Lord and Heavenly Father?" asked the Pastor.

"I do and I will," I replied with broken speech and teary eyes.

He leaned me back and eased me into the icy water. Instead of feeling shocked by the cold, I was flooded with relief. After I was pulled out of the trough, Hatch threw a towel around me and gave me another hug.

Something very powerful and dynamic had just happened. There I was surrounded by some of the baddest men in the state, yet it seemed not to matter what they thought of me, as long as I had forgiveness from God.

In the hobby room, a room designated in Unit Four for hobbies and crafts, I met Ishmael, aka Izzy. Everything he created was wonderful: portraits, pointillism, white charcoal silhouettes on black paper.

"Your art's amazing," I said.

"Oh I don't know about that. But it keeps me busy. Thanks for the compliments."

"I was wondering if we could get paints or art supplies sent in?" I asked.

"No paints or brushes are allowed. They think we will fill the tubes of paint with drugs and smuggle them in. And brushes can be made into shanks. Funny they don't worry about toothbrushes."

He told me we could have pencils or pens, charcoals and pastels along with art paper.

"If you show me some new mediums and the products I need; I will buy you some, too." I said.

"You don't have to do that," he said, adding that he'd be happy to help me.

I told him I wanted to learn how to draw portraits like he did. He handed me a picture of a little girl wearing Osh Kosh Overalls in a cowboy hat that was too big for her, a Xerox copy from a page out of a book. He gave me a few hints about getting the facial features in the right places. Then told me to go work on it. After a little over an hour, I was pleased with my work. When I brought it to him, he looked at it and told me go work on it some more. I came back an hour later with my masterpiece. He glanced at it and said, "Go work on it some more." By the end of the day I came back with the most incredible art I'd ever completed. Once again he looked at it, and repeated, "Go work on it some more." Knowing I really needed help on facial features, he then gave me a book offering lessons on eyes, lips, mouths and noses. I started to realize how hard it is to make a face look real. I learned how to keep going over and over a piece.

Now, most of my creations run me an average of two hundred hours, or more. In an hour Izzy could draw a portrait that would put mine to shame. One day, I was amazed while watching him work on a caricature of himself, Woody, Mike and Hatch playing in their band. In just one hour he'd created a wonderfully exaggerated cartoon. I was in awe. This man was a walking talent.

He told me he was amazed how I could alternate from right to left hand while drawing a picture. Because I have no real dexterity or grip in my right hand, I had to wedge the pencil in between my fingers so it would not slip out. I can't bend my right wrist and hand so I had to learn to use my left hand to make angles that were not possible with my right hand. When doing pointillism sometimes I would be nearly finished after 100 to 200 hours of work, and then the pen would slip out my right hand and make a long mark in the middle of the picture, ruining it. I'd have to start over.

If a picture I drew had a crinkle or a minute flaw, Izzy would crumple it up and toss it at me. And then he'd say something like, "Here, just use this piece of crumpled paper." I learned how to create amazing art because of him. Soon I started sending my art out and also selling it to the prison guards. I used this money to pay for my classes and books for college.

I enjoyed depicting Native American women in pointillism and charcoals. My sister took them to the reservation to sell.

I always had a fascination with Native American art. My aunt and grandmother on my father's side painted in that theme, probably because his father was half Cherokee and half German. I distinctly remember an Indian piece my aunt painted for my mother. It was framed in a gold frame Uncle Bob had soldered. The piece hung at our house on Richards Way. As a kid I would run into the living room to look at it then run back into my room and try to draw it. I could never get past the nose and forehead. I remember my adrenaline would be flowing while doing this. Creativity gave me a high.

The Coach, who ran the gym, was a big guy, not real lean if you know what I mean. More of the Foghorn Leghorn character. Maybe six feet-four inches tall and probably 275 pounds or more. He had dark brown hair and a baby face. I often wondered how he got that job and the respect that went along with it. Many years later I learned his brother was Coconut Dan.

Coconut Dan rode with the Mongols, a one-percent group. A

one-percent motorcycle group is a group of bad asses and outlaws. A black belt, Coconut Dan had been on the Wild World Sports Channel in the early '80s, breaking coconuts with is bare hands. When I learned this, I figured Coach must be a lot more formidable than how he seemed. On Fourth of July and Labor Day weekends he lined up a day of events like sprints, races and weight-lifting competitions. We would be in our groups: whites against Heavy and the blacks, tensions running high. The night before we would meet up and make our plan.

"Be ready for anything. This is when shit kicks off as you well know," Rock would say.

"Beefster, (yes my nickname followed me) we want you to pack." That meant they wanted me to carry the shanks. "You will not be playing in any of the reindeer games. This way we are not all packing during our events."

The morning of the events, we were busy taping magazines around our midsections, protection from potential stabbing. Just hope they don't hit your neck or face. If shit kicked off, I was to hand everyone their piece. My jaw was aching I had it clenched tight throughout the day. I even spit out bits of tooth now and then from the pressure.

The camaraderie of the yard came together, every one cheering, rooting and yelling for their friends to win. As usual, the blacks dominated the track events. However, when it came to the weights we had a very tight competition. During these events we stayed on lookout, because the blacks got very wound up when we won. Baby Hog and Rock were very strong in these events.

Then finally the best part of the day came: one of the very few times we would get real meat. Usually country ribs or some kind of flat iron steaks. Nothing real fancy, but hey, it sure beat a blank.

In the summer you could walk the track outside all day or after dinner until dark. But in the winter we were locked down to our units right after chow because dark fell early. This made for long time. We spent the evenings walking halls in Unit Four. It was one of these nights in winter when Rock, who held a third-degree black belt, had me hold a book over my head as high as possible as he would do a spinning back kick. He slammed that book out of my hand as I held it at least seven feet from the ground. What a stud. But Rock had another side to him: he shot up heroin.

"Hey man, you want some?" he'd ask, slurring his words, his eyes looking like a bloodhound's.

"No, thank you," I always said.

Then the next day Rock could walk out to the yard and squat 405 for tens and bench 405 for sixes. Unreal.

Chapter 15: Unit 7

My days started at 7 a.m. with a very strong cup of instant black coffee, bitter and unpleasant as it were, just like most everything else in prison. I had gotten used to it. Breakfast was fruit and cream Quaker oatmeal. This was to give me the energy I needed for my morning routine, three-mile jog, twelve rounds on the heavy bag followed by 500 sit ups.

At first it had been difficult for me to jog because I weighed 245 pounds, a lot of weight to move. Within six months of boxing I'd dropped forty pounds and was addicted to running. If I missed a day I felt like shit and would pinch my sides to see if I was getting fat! I jogged backwards and sideways, throwing punches the whole way. When I ran with JW, he pushed me until I puked. At 250 pounds, JW moved like a gazelle. Many of the other boxers were professionals; the lightweights and featherweights, never ran. When they fought they knew how to relax in the ring. They were so quick, so fast, they never went many rounds. It was truly baffling to hear the stories about all the smoking and drugs they did as boxers when they were on the outside.

After jogging three miles I gathered my gloves and mouthpiece and did twelve rounds with the heavy bag. I liked to do rounds in sync with the songs on the radio, which served as my timer since most songs are two to three minutes long. During the heavy bag training I pictured either Worm, Spot or at times Butch. This pumped up my adrenaline and gave me the extra energy to complete the last few rounds.

It took me about a year to get pretty good on the bag. While I was working out on the bag there would be between 500-750 other prisoners on the yard doing their thing. As usual there was always someone, usually a black dude that would pop off, "That bag don't hit back." I would wave him on over but he never took me up on my offer.

Now it was time to visit the iron pile for my 500 sit-ups. Plus, another 20-30 minutes of leg raises and abdominals, and then the medicine ball to get those abs tight. I loved that ball. I wanted to develop a muscle down in my lower abs so I could take punches to the midsection. You get in pretty good shape throwing a 25 lb. leather ball at someone's stomach and then they in turn toss it back at you. This went on for about twenty minutes. By then it was time for lock-down for lunch. While in lock-down waiting for lunch, I'd work on my homework for my evening college classes.

I was building my self-esteem through self-discipline by setting goals, reaching them and sometimes exceeding them. College initially took a great deal of mental effort. I asked God to help me overcome my learning disabilities. I had to discipline my mind and re-learn how to study. Math courses were especially hard for me. But when I applied myself it became a piece of cake. Just like anything else. I became addicted to studying as much as running and learning the Lord's word. My GPA went from .08 to 3.85 and I was on the Dean's honor list every semester. This was positive fuel.

After chow, I'd set up the weights. Two to three hours a day on weights does wonders to the human body. Two years earlier my arm felt like it would snap with a 2.5 pound dumbbell. Now I could do curls with a 75-pounder. I was doing 405-pound front squats and hitting 315 lbs. on back squats for thirty-five reps.

Some days, Ziggy and I would hang out on the weight pile watching the new fish. I watched a fish hit a couple hundred pounds on the squats. He would be straining to hit a few reps then rack the bar like a stud.

"Hey man, that's pretty good." I said.

"Yeah, that's a lot of weight," he replied.

"Takes a lot of balls to get under that kind of weight," I would say with a half-smile on my face. "But hell with tree trunks legs like those you should be banging out twice that weight."

"Shit I'd like to see you do that."

"Not sure I can," I said earnestly. "Maybe for a pizza or a couple milk shakes for my dog and me, I can try 315 pounds for thirty-five reps."

"No way, and if you don't?" he asked.

"Pizza and shakes for you and your dog."

Ziggy and I would throw a plate on each side of the bar for me. I would bang out ten reps nice and slow.

Then we would add a plate to each side, I would get back under it and bang out twenty reps, a little quicker this time. This is where the smiles faded from their faces. We then put 315 pounds on the bar, three plates each side, and I would bang out 35 reps.

No one ever argued over payment.

Years later, on the outside, I won a few steak and lobster dinners at one of the gyms with this same bet.

After weights it would be back to the cell to finish homework for the next classes. I was taking upper division Psychology, Anatomy, Physiology and fun classes like Statistics, which we named Sadistics. It was very rewarding to see what kind of scores I could make with a little effort. If I could I would try to squeeze a little nap in before dinner.

One time in the chow line, I was chatting it up with a guard I liked named Higgins. Like me, he was a body builder; he helped us to get a line of vitamins and supplements into the prison.

"Helm," he said, "just do me a favor. If anything ever kicks off, please do not come after me. Most of these idiot officers have no idea what kind of shape some of you guys are in. I watch you run three miles every day, twelve rounds on the heavy bag, then abs, weights, and then boxing in the evenings. Hell you must work out eight hours a day."

I grinned; pleased he seemed to respect my work ethic.

"But really, Helm, don't ever come at me. I would have to shoot you to stop you."

"Don't worry," I said. "I would never come for you. I would go after an asshole, like Pizza Face or Little Kenny"

We laughed.

About once a week a few of us gathered to box. I would box with blacks, whites, Mexicans and Indians. One day I was boxing a mountain of a man. He was huge, weighing in at 265 pounds and not an ounce of fat. I had just lost forty pounds and this made me quicker. But this man was a southpaw, which meant I had to move in the opposite directions than what I'd trained for or was used to. If not, I'd get knocked out by walking into his left. He ended up hitting me so hard it felt as though he had knocked my teeth out the back of my neck. I thought I surely must have lost my front teeth. Fortunately, that hadn't happened but I couldn't open my jaw for a while. I lived on milk and shakes for that month.

In prison you can't be denied your religious beliefs or practices. The incarcerated Native Americans had a sweat lodge along with a dipping pool to cool off in. After I had mentioned to them my grandfather was half Cherokee, my Native America boxing buddies James and JW along with Franco, Big Ray and Harley, invited me to start joining them in their sweat, followed eating Indian tacos for their religious services. The focus was being one with nature and becoming a more enlightened individual.

Now picture a one square mile radius, with a ground of decomposed granite no trees or plant life surrounded by concrete buildings. To the northwest side, under a guards' tower, was a little place known as the Indians' area. This was the only place on the yard that had actual dirt, which enabled them to grow melons, jalapeños and tomato plants, a lush green area that provided respite from the bleakness of the yard. Harley watered and tended to the plants and the area. The sweat lodge frame was covered with prison blankets. Inside was a fire pit for the rocks and just outside sat the dipping pool for after the sweat. Before I was ever invited to join in, I walked by like everyone else and envied that little area. To those of us stuck on the hot, dry desolate dismal yard this appeared like a small oasis, a moment to forget where you really were.

We built a big fire and heated up many large rocks to create a dry sauna. With every round Harley would add water to the hot rocks and start the steam. He sprinkled sage and pine so the scent filled the lodge. We then rubbed the smoke into our skin for purification. We sat or lay down to do as many rounds as we could tolerate. Initially I could only handle one to two, but later I worked up to seven and eight rounds right along with Ray, Jeffery, Franco and Harley. We stumbled out of there right before we passed out from heat exhaustion and lay in the dipping pool. Such a luxury, like being downtown instead of prison. The prison supplied us with real meat and fry bread dough. We had all the necessary ingredients for making a pot of beans, a pot of rice and a pan of fried potatoes. We also had hamburger or real meat to fry. We'd make two salsas, a raw one and a cooked one. The other prisoners hung on the fence, mouths watering, until the guards yelled for them to move along. We ate until we were so full we couldn't possibly take another bite. We split up the left over tacos and shared them. Jeffrey and I walked out of there with five or six tacos we could use for bartering.

While we were enjoying our summer camp activities, the prison system built a nice new modern Unit Seven out the back of the yard. Compared to the old cells that were at least twenty or thirty years old, this new modern building was like the Hilton.

While the women's prison was being renovated the women were transferred to this new unit until theirs was completed. As we walked the yard after meals and during the day, we tried to get the women's attention by smiling and talking to them through the chain-link fence. Some of the men hadn't seen a woman in many years. It was like watching a documentary on the Discovery or Animal Planet on apes and baboons and their mating rituals. It was quite comical at times. The guys were dancing around like kids at play on a school yard. Then the guards yelled at us to get away from the fence or to move along.

One day I noticed a woman with nice long blond flowing hair coupled with a nice lean body. As I walked by each lap I noticed her noticing me. On one lap, I showed her the number three with my hand. The next lap, I showed her a five well four and a half, I was missing half my thumb. But she got it. Each time she nodded until she had all the digits to my sister's phone number. Later she called my sister and exchanged addresses, and we began to write each other.

Her name was Tonya and she was down for prostitution. I didn't care. I was just happy to have a woman to chat with.

Once the women were moved back to their prison, Unit Four was transferred to the Hilton.

As we walked in the new unit, we were in awe; it was so modern, nice and clean. The twenty-foot high ceilings made it feel vastly roomier and lighter than the eight-foot ceilings of the old units. The cells had nice beds and even a desk that would fold down from the wall. Perfect for the new Brother word processor I had purchased to complete my psychology term papers. The floors were shiny and clean, the windows tinted. The peace and quiet of the new place was more conducive to studying. Morale definitely improved.

The only disadvantage was that the showers were positioned right in front of the guards' station, no walls no windows, just right out in the open. I had to get used to taking showers that way, especially in front of the several female correctional officers. I assumed they were embarrassed to have to sit there and watch us shower. Maybe some actually enjoyed it?

When you are down and a cute girl in a miniskirt comes to visit you, you savor every moment and enjoy it fully. Her name was Ronda, a friend from beauty college. She had learned from my sister I was in prison and that I was getting divorced. We had started writing and then we had her processed so she could visit, which she did often.

When Betty learned of Ronda's visits, she told my sister she had made a huge mistake and wanted to reunite with me. Betty had learned what we all previously knew. Spot was not the great catch. He was an alcoholic.

I only had to sign the divorce papers one more time, and we were done. I wanted nothing to do with her, but she asked to visit and I allowed it. Wearing her shortest of short miniskirts, Betty knew how to get me. After nearly three years of being down, she was hard to resist. When I saw her walk in the visiting room, I felt the old feelings of love and lust that had drawn me to her. Her long slender legs, tiny waist and butt, along with her long flowing blond hair, coupled with her innocent smile. I started to melt. We hugged and found a private area to sit and talk.

"Oh Beef, you're looking so good," she said. "I'm so sorry for what I've done."

"Right, how's Sancho or Spot?" I asked with a cocky attitude.

"He's disgusting; he drinks until he passes out almost every night. It was fun to party with him at first but then it got old soon. I want us to start over."

"I don't know Betty," I said. "I'm not sure I care for you anymore." I lied through my teeth, wanting her to feel a little of the pain she made me feel. I wanted her to squirm and see how she reacted. Maybe she'd just get pissed off and go back to Spot.

"Please Beef, I'll do anything you want. I thought I could wait, but I got caught up in the party scene and started to drink because I was bored and depressed."

"Really, how do you think I felt?" I started to get annoyed at her. She had no idea what I was going through. She wasn't there for me.

"Please let me come back and show you that I'm serious."

"I don't need you. I have put all my efforts into my schooling, health and spirituality. I am not the same guy you once knew. In fact, I go to my parole hearing in three months. I'm also nearly complete with an Associated in Arts in Psychology. I have made Deans Honor list almost every semester. If I work it right, I will get my parole and an A.A. within the next few months."

"Please let me try. I will not disappoint you."

"What if I get a two or three-year dump, what then?"

"I'll behave and wait for you, I promise. Just let me know what you want me to do."

"Really? Okay then, this is what I want, I just don't care anymore about us. I actually have someone coming to visit me now and I have known her for many more years than you. You will go to Spot's house, get your things and you will be at Lucy's ranch before eight tonight. You can stay in one of the cabins. I don't care that there is no heat, and it is a very inconvenient for you. You will commute to and from work even though it is an hour drive each way, home by 6 p.m. every night. There will be no staying in town on Friday nights and you will spend the weekends at the ranch. Take it or leave it."

"I'll be there tonight. Call me at eight if you can get to a phone."

I kissed her and told her I loved her and missed her. This brought tears to both our eyes.

She prattled on about how easy this would be for her.

I reluctantly told Ronda to stop coming to see me.

My parole date was finally here. There I sat at a long table in front of three people, a gray-haired gentleman, an African American women and a white nun. We were in a room I hadn't seen my whole three years in prison. With my hair cut short, I was dressed in prison blues (blue jeans and a blue denim shirt) and my black and green Adidas I had purchased for boxing. My skin prickled with nerves, but I tried to relax. I had to keep my composure.

"Mr. Helm, how are you?" the man asked.

"I'm wonderful, thank you for asking. And yourselves?" I asked.

"We're fine, thank you for asking."

"If there is one thing you have learned during your time in prison," said the nun, "please tell us what it is."

"I have learned that no one but me got me into this situation," I said with conviction. "I blame no one but myself."

"Very good, sir," said the nun. "Tell us what you have done to rehabilitate yourself."

"It has been a long road to rehabilitation," I said. I explained how, after finishing my high school diploma my first year, I was about to receive an A.A. in Psychology with a 3.85 GPA. I added that I'd made Deans honor list almost every semester and that I'd attended N.A. every Saturday for three years.

"I don't see myself ever doing cocaine again, let alone selling it. I have tried to educate myself in order to earn an honest living."

"Yes we've noticed you've worked very hard and we congratulate you on your efforts. What are your plans if you do receive a parole from us today?"

"Due to my hand injuries, I still have vocational training and or schooling coming from the state. I'm planning on requesting schooling for x-ray or Ultrasound, if permitted."

"Very good," said the African American woman. "We do see a positive change in you. This is actually refreshing for us to see."

Before I left, I shook their hands and thanked them for their time. I walked out feeling there's no way I could have done it better.

The next few weeks seemed to drag by. I was doing anything and everything to keep my mind busy. It was hard to concentrate on art and homework at first, but as the days passed by the excitement faded and the routine came back to me. I had learned to hope for the best, but expect the worse.

I was in the hobby room working on a pastel of a Big Buck picture for a guard when I heard the guard yell, "Helm get over here you have mail!" An interdepartmental envelope, meaning it was from the prison. My hands shanking, I tore opened the letter.

Parole. I'd gotten my parole.

All my work had finally paid off.

Parole, though, was no guarantee I was going to get out. A jealous prisoner can fuck up the whole thing for someone who's about ready to be released. Many guys short on time will not go out to chow or even the yard the closer they get to their parole date. Like them I started to buy all my food from the commissary and go to the yard to work out when it was not so crowded. I made sure wherever and whenever I went out I had a dog on my back for protection. I wasn't about to jeopardize the freedom I was about to taste.

Two months from my parole date, I explained to my professors of Creative Writing, Anatomy, Macro business, and Business Psychology that I would be out on parole, or could be out on parole before finishing the classes. They agreed to give me my homework and finals in advance so I could complete the semester before I got out.

Less than a week away from my parole, I was feeling so proud of myself. I had beaten prison. I had made something of my time and myself. I had found God and accomplished a tremendous amount of goals. I felt satisfied. Happy, even. Big John and Ziggy came by my cell asking if I wanted to go to chow

"Not really. I don't want to take a chance."

They assured me nothing would go wrong. They had my back. How can you tell your dogs no to that?

While standing in line, Higgins and I bullshitted a little and I quietly let him know I was on my way out. With a big smile he looked at me and congratulated me.

As I worked my way through the chow line, I got to the last man serving food, a small toad with a cocky smirk on his face.

He tossed a small portion of mashed potatoes on my plate letting it drip down the side. Then he just stood there looking at me, as I shook my plate at him, a well-known signal meaning I wanted more.

"Fuck you, cracker!" he yelled. "Don't tell me what to do, you're a prisoner just like me!"

"What did you say?" I asked, with temper rising quickly.

"I said fuck you. You don't tell me what to do!" he replied.

A guy behind the counter who knew me jumped in.

"Man you better just shut up and give him some more, he boxes daily. He'll knock your black ass out!"

"I'll fuck you up, cracker!" yelled the tiny toad while throwing down the spoon.

"Shut your trap!" warned Higgins. "Give him another scoop now!"

When Big John, Ziggy and I sat down, I was fuming. Just what I was trying to avoid. Now I had to squash this, or be deemed a punk.

I lay awake all night, adrenaline flowing like it had not in years, trying to make my plan. I had to hang out of sight and catch him unaware. Maybe I'd sock him up, meaning, put a pad lock in a sock and wail on his head. I was mad at myself. I knew better than going to chow this late in the game. I knew I was supposed to be Christian now. Turn the other cheek and all that. But sometimes, in prison you have to react to an external stimulus in a non-Christian manner. At least that's how I justified it to myself. I was in prison. The rules were the rules: getting punked was the worst thing I could do. I knew I needed to behave to get out, but getting out was the future. Right now was what mattered. Lying in a pool of sweat, I knew I had no choice. I had to squash this.

The next morning, Big John showed up with a big smile on his face. Not saying a word he shoved a $100 store list in my hand.

"What's this John?"

"It's a store list for you to fill out from the toad in the kitchen. He sends his apologies. He wants nothing to do with you."

"Really." *Thank God*, I thought.

"The boys from the kitchen showed me where he bunked. They had explained to him who you were," John said. "As I walked up to him he started back peddling, asking what you were going to do about it. I told him you're probably going to use him as a heavy bag, shank him or sock him up, but I let him know, he's not walking away." He asked me what he should do. I said for starters a hundred-dollar store order would work." John looked at me with his big shit-eating grin.

Relief softened me. I smiled, "Thank you."

"It's the least I could do. I talked you into going to eat."

The day finally came. I left my Brother word processor with James and wished him the best of luck in school. I left various clothes and my lifting gear with the people I thought needed them the most. And most the stuff I bought with the hundred-dollar store list, a couple cases of tuna, ice cream, and popcorn, I gave to Big John.

Believe it or not for a moment, it was a sad feeling leaving that place. Knowing I probably would never again meet people so dedicated that they are willing to die with you over such petty matters as one's pride. At the same time, I couldn't wait to get out, knowing there were people in there willing to kill you over the same. Pride.

What a memory riding through the yard one last time in the guard's golf cart with my yellow tub. I remembered my first days standing on the one-square mile yard wondering, *How am I going to do this? Will the day ever come when I get to leave?* When my friends like Hoffur and Neil from Unit Three, were released I felt left behind, sure that my day would never come.

How many good memories I had accumulated in such a nasty place. I made it only because I had accepted the Lord into my life. He gave me the strength, the wisdom and the passion to succeed.

As I passed by the guard towers and ominous razor wire, a tear tried to well up. I fought it back.

A few guys in the chow line, Big Ray and Franco, raised their hands yelling, "Stay down Beef, good luck."

Stay down, stay solid, and don't change.

Chapter 16: Fresh Out

Betty stood at the gate, her hair shining in the sun. My angel. My sexy angel, wearing her brown leather miniskirt with fish net stockings and pumps.

I pulled her to me, feeling her familiar curves, kissing her eager lips. Feelings I forgot existed swam through my blood. I was grateful we had overcome our difficulties.

We climbed into her car. My parents were expecting us, a thirty-minute drive. It was awkward to be in a car, riding down the road. The movement felt odd. Everything looked so big and open. How strange to see people not wearing blue or pickle green, people who could decide to turn the car right or left on a whim.

It was all I could do to sit in my seat and keep my hands off my wife. I was like a dog being teased with a bone, frothing at the mouth.

Half way to my parents' house, our primal urges took over. We pulled over at the State Park Lake to a secluded area under some big cottonwoods. It was as exciting, if not more, than my first time. We felt like two teenagers doing the forbidden before Mom and Dad got home.

Five years of parole lay ahead of me. When I met with my parole officer, a young guy with slicked-back hair who looked like an Italian mobster, I told him I planned to be in school full time.

"That's great," he said. "Just one thing. Nothing better happen to Butch or Worm, or you're going back to prison."

"No problem," I said. I'd planned to steer clear of my old friends, or anyone who knew those guys. I wanted to start over and to hang out with successful people, not guys who had nothing better to do than settle, working construction, drinking and smoking their lives away. There would not be any great love loss.

A few days later, I attended graduation. I had the opportunity to walk with Western Nevada Community College within a few weeks of my parole. I was wearing my blue cap and gown getting ready to walk down the aisle. My parents were so proud. I had to keep stopping what I was doing so my mother could snap snap snap a million photos. I was the only person in my immediate family that had even attended college, let alone from inside the prison walls.

As I walked down the aisle to receive my diploma, a surreal feeling swept over me. Just two weeks before the only people surrounding me were felons, murderers, rapist, and strong-arm robbers. Now, the positive energy of the regular law-abiding folks uplifted me.

Once I learned it would take another five years to achieve a graduate degree in psychology, I decided to study radiology, x-ray or Ultrasound like I had previously envisioned before I was sent away. It would take less time; I would make good money. I had experienced so many x-rays, and had taken many anatomy and physiology courses, and knew the body well because of all my accidents and being a body builder,

I figured I could breeze through radiography study.

At a workers' comp meeting, the counselor was impressed with my dedication to school work in prison. Soon I learned that my worker's comp industrial insurance vocational training would pay for my three years of schooling. This would set a precedent for the state. If I could pull it off, they would continue to offer this program to anyone with my extent of disability and dedication for higher learning. My head whirled with gratitude.

I had one more obstacle to contend with. I still had to meet with the people in charge of the x-ray schooling to see if they thought I could physically handle the job. And, more importantly, as an ex-felon, could I be licensed? I was assured there would be no problem, since it was a non-violent victim-less crime.

Just a few months out and I had everything lined up for my future. In the mornings, I did my homework. I had to re-read each chapter several times, highlighting as I went. I made flash cards, which I looked at throughout the day. The rest of my time was spent going to school and the gym.

Soon, Betty told me she wanted to move back to Oregon. She missed her family. We were having a difficult time getting along. She liked to drink, and when she drank she got very feisty and argumentative; and then if I had a drink, too, it was double trouble. I would go out with Big Dave sometimes to the country nightclub down the street. Probably not a good idea, to not invite Betty. However, since she had three years to go play, I figured I should be allowed out once in a while with my friends. She would show up at the club and start an argument. It didn't take much to light her fuse and once lit, it was impossible to extinguish.

I figured it might be a good idea to for us to talk to my old psychology teacher Dr. Kulick who owned her own counseling business. Part of me still resented Betty cheating on me with Spot. I knew I had to put this behind me or it would never work. I figured I would take the first step and made an appointment with Dr. Kulick. I explained to her what we were going through. She asked me to see if Betty would go through some couples counseling with me. But Betty wouldn't go.

"Maybe," I said to Dr. Kulick, "I should go to Oregon. I feel a little bit guilty. I mean, she waited for me."

"She didn't wait for you very well," Dr. Kulick said. "You should do what will make you the happiest."

I wanted to stay and finish my schooling, she wanted to go back to Oregon. After a couple more blowouts, we decided to get a divorce. I had a pain in my heart, but I also knew I had already taken her back once. That was only six months ago. She knew what I still needed to achieve to be finished with school and make a decent living, which was my goal. Obviously not *our* goal. I decided I had to just let her go and continue working on my future. Betty would move back to Oregon, and soon marry an old high school sweetheart of hers.

With the settlement from my right-hand disability ratings of amputation of the right hand, I purchased a house in August of 1993. My best friend Big Dave's mother, Michelle, was a Realtor who found me a fixer upper in the very neighborhood I lived in as a child. It was surrounded by luscious yards full of mature fruit trees: cherry, apple, peach and apricot. Perennial flowers lined the edges of that yard with something different blooming each week all summer long. When I saw the covered patio surrounded by grapevines, I knew it was the perfect place to put a hot tub. I envisioned soaking in the hot water, pulling grapes off the vine. I was imagining myself laying out on a blanket in the back yard, studying in my personal paradise.

Big Dave and I spent many a day remodeling the house. Pulling up the carpets, we discovered natural hardwood floors. These had to be sanded and sealed, and the base boards replaced, due to all the dog and cat urine that had soaked through the carpets from many years of neglect. The walls had to be sanded down because of the layers of residual smoke and grime, along with re-sheet rocking the walls to rid them of old disgusting wall paper. We found it is much easier to throw up quarter inch dry wall over them and re-texture rather than trying to remove the paper. Once finished it looked and smelled like a new home.

Our neighbors asked how the remodel was coming. I invited them in for a walk-through.

As I described the changes Big Dave and I made, I said, "I'd never seen a more disgusting house! The people who lived here were slobs and smoked. It was so despicable, even the walls had rings around the pictures from the smoke"

When they left, Big Dave said, "Hey, man did you realize you were talking to the people who used to rent here?"

Oh crap. I felt like such a schmuck.

Chapter 17: I Street

In my little house on I Street, I spent most of my time either studying at the kitchen table or outside on the lawn catching rays. There were always five or six books spread out on the table, alongside a package of fluorescent highlighters and flashcards. Many weekends, people would call to see if I wanted to go to the lake with my boat or go motorcycle riding, but my answer was no, most the time.

I was fascinated by how well my methods of learning were working. It seemed I had the highest GPA in the x-ray class, and I'd hand in my tests and quizzes long before anyone else. Many students wanted to study with me. I quickly learned studying with one other person was best. More people than that, the afternoon would devolve into a bullshit session.

My friend Jim got me a job as a bouncer for a nightclub in Reno called Scruples. A heavyset guy with blond hair and blue eyes, he looked just like the baby on the jars of baby food. I called him Gerber. The club was one of the most popular after hours' clubs around, with great looking waitresses always wearing cute little shorts and big smiles. Scruples was known for their great food and good prices. Jim and I knew the cooks well and they always kept us filled with their delicious hot wings. Because there was always a bountiful array of good-looking women trolling the place, it was easy to find a date to take on the boat the next day. One night I noticed a fellow student from x-ray class walk in. She saw me and approached me. Spring had red hair that you could see a mile away. She looked Irish, but she was Latina with red hair and freckles.

"Hi there," said Spring. "I think you are in my x-ray class aren't you?"

"Why yes, yes I am," I replied.

"You seem to have no problem handing your tests and quizzes long before the rest of the class."

"I study very hard," I said, pleased that she had noticed. "Usually for most of the day."

"Would you like to take on a study partner?" she asked.

"I'm not sure. I've tried the study group thing. It always turns into a bullshit session."

"That wouldn't happen. It would be just me. I need help."

"I tell you what. You are pretty cute." I smiled. So did she. "Let's give it a try for a few times and see how it goes."

"God, that would be great. I won't disappoint you, I promise."

Spring and I made great head way. We soon had a system down of using my flashcards as quiz questions. If you could answer the flash cards, you could answer the questions on the quizzes and tests.

Once we got to know each other there was a sense of flirtation developed. I had a girlfriend at the time, so I never pushed pass the flirting. However, after a few semesters, there seemed to be an unavoidable attraction building between us. A few classmates teased us that they were sure more than just studying going on.

Then I had a great idea one night. I suggested maybe we should start playing strip study. I asked Spring what she thought about the idea, and she jumped at it.

"So Spring, what is the other name for scatter radiation?" I asked.

"Shit, I know the answer to this one, I just can't remember it."

"Beep, wrong answer, Spring," I happily said.

As she pulled her shirt off exposing her sheer green bra, I could tell she had a very nice and tight body.

"In the lower extremity, which bone is smaller, tibia, or fibula?"

"Tibia."

"Beep, wrong answer again."

Soon she was just sitting there in just her panties, and I was missing a few articles of clothing, too. As fun as it was, neither one of us wanted to be the first to lose all our clothes. I think we were both afraid of what would happen next if we got completely naked. It was all I could do to maintain myself and keep getting the questions right.

As hard as we tried to behave ourselves, one night we ended up in the hot tub naked. Before long we had splashed most of the water out of the Jacuzzi and needed to take our passion to the room. We had built up many months of lust and curiosity for each other, and I could tell it was well worth the wait. However, we never went all the way. I was always involved with someone else, and just did not want to have that hanging over my head.

In addition to my days of classes, I interned at the various hospitals in the area. I was enamored with all the technology and equipment in the hospital: the cool x-ray machines and hardware, the MRI and CT. Each hospital had different equipment and different procedures and protocols.

I very much enjoyed working surgery and trauma x-ray. In surgery I was so worried about breaking the sterile barrier and not contaminating anything, the time flew by. However, during cauterization, the aroma of burning flesh and tissue was nauseating.

Trauma was very fast paced and high pressure, working on people fresh off the street. Working nights, especially Halloween and even full moons was wild. When a drunk and belligerent patient spit blood at me and tried to hit me, I learned how to stay professional and get the job done. The last patient I x-rayed in trauma had been hit by a bus. Even though he was dead, I had to x-ray his broken bones. Every time I moved a body part, blood flowed over my shoes and me. By the end of the exam, I was covered from head to toe in his blood. That is when I started to realize, *they don't pay me enough to do this.*

Sadie was an older Spanish woman, barely five feet tall with graying dark curly hair and a tinge of an accent. She knew the trade well and made for a great on-site instructor. She taught with Marylou, tall and pale with blond curly hair, in her forties. They were employed by the hospital and their job seemed more or less to make sure students didn't hurt or kill anyone. At first they weren't very friendly.

"Go get that room ready for a BE," they would bark.

"Can you show me how?"

"You students really need to be more prepped before you step foot into this hospital," Sadie said. "Marylou and I do not have time to babysit you guys all day!"

"It really pisses me off," said Marylou. "They expect us to do our jobs and hold your hands all day."

However, if you learned fast and were not lazy, they would warm right up to you.

My second year, Sadie was diagnosed with cancer. She stayed working as long as she could. In her early fifties, she was full of spunk and vigor even though she was sick. She always had that little sparkle in her eye and sometimes a big smile spread across her face. When her hair started to get patchy due to chemo, she had a conversation with

Marylou that I overheard.

"I sure hate having to go to the salon," she said. "When I take my wig off everyone looks at me funny."

"Oh Sadie don't let that bother you. You have enough to worry about right now. You're going to beat this!"

"I know, but it feels strange to have people look at me. I'm not use to not having hair, especially in clumps, I look horrible."

I came out of the x-ray room.

"Sadie, I'm a hairdresser. You just tell me when you want your hair cut, and I'll cut it right here in one of the rooms for you. No charge. It will be my pleasure for the all the times you and Marylou have helped me."

"Really, you would do that for me?"

"In a heartbeat!"

She smiled, hugged me and thanked me.

From that point on I was her new hairdresser. Sadly, Sadie would pass from that bout with cancer. RIP, my friend.

Working in Fluoroscopy, x-ray in motion was very interesting. I performed barium studies, like upper GIs and small bowel follow-through. After giving the patients a chocolate, vanilla or strawberry barium shake to drink, I'd roll them on the table and take x-rays of their upper gastric system and small bowels. If they could not ingest barium due to allergies or some other reason, they would have to drink Gastrographin, which is so bitter some people would vomit it right back up.

Then came the day I had to tip someone for a barium enema, which involves inserting the tip of the of the tube into the patient's rectum. I hated dealing with strangers' butts so much that I thought, I'd rather be out digging a ditch. I couldn't see me doing this very often and still enjoying my work. One female patient didn't mind tipping herself. I only wished all my patients could be as accommodating.

It just so happened that when I went to class the next day, I met some people from Loma Linda University who were there to review our school's accreditation. I asked one of them if they taught other modalities at Loma Linda. Smiling at me, the man told me yes, they taught ultra sound, MRI, CT and nuclear medicine. I gave him my name and address, and asked him if he would be as kind as to send me some literature for those programs. He seemed more than happy to do so.

Later at the desk of the radiology supervisor, I saw a plaque that read:

X-ray tech-$12.00/hr.

MRI tech-$13.00/hr.

CT tech-$14.00/hr.

Ultra sound tech-$15.00/hr.

Nuclear medicine tech-$17.00/hr.

It was then I knew what I wanted to do.

Ending the second year of x-ray school, I felt great. I was working out five days a week and doing well in school and my internships.

Recalling how big and strong Butch was, and how once he'd pierced the skin he didn't feel the needle, I started using steroids, or as he'd said, waging chemical warfare on the body. I was already huge and in great shape, but I wanted to see how much bigger and stronger I could get. I did my research: equipoise burned fat as did testosterone, which also made you strong. There was Deca Durabolin, which put on size and increased the synovial fluid in your joints and help keep them lubed. Then every one's favorite: Sustanon 250, which greatly increased strength.

The stronger you are, the more weight you can lift. The more weight you lift, the more muscle tissue breaks down, and the more weight your central nervous system can handle. The more muscle tissue you break down, the more it is built back up bigger and stronger. Androgenic steroids, like testosterones, burn fat and make you stronger. With the use of anabolic steroids protein is synthesized into muscle tissue much quicker than the body's normal process. So, when combining androgenic and anabolic steroids, you become bigger and stronger much more quickly than normal. Injectables are easier on the liver than the orals. But you had to cycle them, eight weeks on, eight weeks off, so as not to lose your testes. I soon learned this all becomes very addicting. When you're in such great shape, every time you lift you feel how tight, big and hard your muscles are, you can practically watch them grow. Then you want more. Also, you have to start to consume at least two grams of protein for every pound of body weight in order to stay anabolic. This gets very expensive. Not only that, you can only synthesize 50 grams of protein at a time. So, if you weighed 250 pounds like I did, you had to eat ten meals a day two hours apart. This is why it seems a serious body builder is constantly eating all day long.

I had a great relationship with my new parole officer, Riggs. Short and fat, he was always out of breath and sweating,

"For every pound you get me to lose," he once told me. "I'll knock a month off of your parole."

Too bad he was only kidding.

For the most part, I was the ideal parolee, working hard and keeping my life on track.

I did, though, have a close call. After work one night at my bouncer job, I headed up to a nightclub in downtown to see if any of my friends were off work yet. As I was walking into the nightclub, I saw a strawberry blond named Cindy, whom I had met the weekend before at a western dance club. Cindy had a huge smile with big white beautiful teeth and dazzling hazel eyes. Her body was rock hard and quite shapely even after two kids. We decided to go have a few drinks.

Even though I was a body builder and using steroids, I did like to drink a lot. When you do your cycles on 'roids, you shouldn't drink. It's hard on your liver. However, I was a product of Fallon, Nevada. In high school the favorite past time of the local boys is to drink beer and, especially, Jack Daniels. Not just a casual drink here and there. More like a competition. You either kept up or would be deemed a pussy. And as a football player and wrestler, that was unacceptable. In high school it was common for us to pound down 20 to 30 shots of Jack each and then climb in the car and go tear it up downtown. And the hard drinking continued into our adulthood. In fact, by this time, Joe (my high school buddy who had gone to law school while I went to prison) and I could easily sit at a bar and order a Jack and coke, then a Cutty Sark, a Johnnie Walker Red, his brothers Blackie and Blue, too, then a martini and sure a margarita sounds good, let's follow that up with a Jim Beam to boot, oh wait, I think I need a shot of tequila or Jack for the road. Let's wash it down with an ice cold beer. Each drink would never last us more than two or three minutes. It was no problem for us to pound down ten to fifteen drinks in a half hour or less. When we would close the bar at nights as bouncers, the bartenders knew to just start pouring drinks and not stop until we told them. We only had thirty minutes or so get our buzz on, and get our buzz on is just what we did well. The thought that this may be a problem never really occurred to me. I used booze as an equalizer to my adrenaline. The more my adrenaline flowed, the more liquor I would pound down, the more I pounded down, the more my adrenaline flowed.

Cindy was cocky, but beautiful. I liked her smile, her attitude. I could easily fall for her. After an evening of drinking and chatting, we went to breakfast as was the custom for Reno, a 24-hour town; when everyone leaves the nightclubs, they seek out the $1.99 casino breakfast specials. As we talked, we discovered we had a number of mutual friends.

She told me she'd recently gotten divorced from a highway patrolman and recently moved back from Las Vegas. I considered myself lucky to be one of the first to meet up with her since her divorce. We made plans to go out the next night.

At 4 a.m., I headed home alone in my Chevy Blazer, which had a huge lift kit coupled with 38-inch tires. My head was still buzzed from the alcohol running through my veins. On a side street near my home, I cut a corner on a left hand turn and nearly sliced the nose off a local city police car.

Oh shit, red lights flashed in my rear-view mirror. If I got a DUI, my parole would be revoked. I'd been out three years only two more to go. I was screwed.

The cop, an older gentleman with graying hair, asked me to please step out of my vehicle.

"Good evening, you almost tore the front end off of my car there," said the cop.

Shaking in my shoes, I tried to speak without slurring my words. I was so nervous I was trembling.

"Yes sir, I am sorry sir, I took that corner a little close. I am just tired, just got off work bouncing at Los Tres, and trying to get home to bed."

"Is that alcohol I smell?" he asked.

"Yes sir, it could be, I had a beer a couple hours ago. I did have breakfast at the Peppermill before getting in my truck, though." I hoped I was speaking convincingly.

"Oh really, well let's try a few tests here and see how you do."

He had me do a few toe to toes, and lean my head back and touch my nose with both hands. I thought I did pretty well.

"My computer says you just got out of prison and are on parole, is that right?"

"Yes sir, that is correct." Nervousness pricked my skin. So much was at stake.

"I can see you don't need any trouble right now."

"No sir, I don't. I'll be graduating from x-ray school in a matter of months." I wondered if that would still be true. Maybe I'd be back behind bars.

"Wait here." The officer headed back to his car.

As I waited, I sweated it out, imagining him telling me to put my hands behind my back and once again, assume the position. My stomach climbed into my mouth. How was I going to make the call to my parents or sister for bail? Oh wait, that's right, there would be no bail. It would be straight back to prison to wait for a hearing there.

"I see you only live a few blocks from here," said the officer when he returned.

"Yes sir, I almost made it."

"Tell you what I am going to do for you. Give me your keys. I will leave them in your mailbox. They will be there waiting for you when you get home."

I couldn't believe it. What a break. I thanked God for this huge favor as I walked home.

It was finally the last day of the academic year. I had one final left, radiation physics. I was sunbathing in the backyard studying my flash cards and flipping through my notes. What a great three years this had been. I was physically and mentally at my peak with all the studying and working out I'd been doing. Through self-discipline, I'd increased my self-confidence dramatically. I felt amazing and was thrilled I was about to graduate.

As I turned the page in my notebook, I saw in capitals at the top of the page something I'd written on the first day of class:

THE FINAL WILL BE BETWEEN 10 A.M. AND 12 P.M.

A memory flooded through me: the first day of radiation physics,

Ma Baker, the instructor, had told us to write down that the final would be held earlier than the usual time of the class. That was the first thing I had written down that day followed by days, weeks, a semester of pages and pages of notes.

I looked down at my watch. Holy shit! It was 11:10 a.m. The final was almost over! I was naked in my backyard and a good twenty-five-minute drive from school. That would give me about twenty minutes to complete the two-hour final on radiation physics.

If I flunked, I was screwed. It was a two-year program, so the class would not be offered for another two years, which in effect would get me kicked off industrial insurance and I would not get to graduate. The last three years would have been for nothing.

I ran through the house like a jack rabbit, throwing on a pair of shorts a tank top and pair of tennis shoes, trying to swallow the lump in the back of my throat.

I burned rubber all the way to the college and came flying around the corner panting like a dog, sweating like a pig. Ma Baker the instructor looked up at me with a slight grin while sitting in a chair outside the door. I had twenty minutes exactly.

I prayed for this to be the time my eight hours of studying a day would pay off.

"Test please," I asked her with my hand held out.

"Are you sure?" she asked concerned.

"No problem, I've got it handled."

Most of the students were still there, heads down, taking the test. A few looked up at me and sighed or shook their heads as I squeezed by. I noticed Chris and Spring were already gone.

When I sat down and started to read the questions, magic kicked in. I knew the answers long before I reached the end of the question. I was trained to read the entire question when taking a tests, but I had two hundred questions to complete in fifteen minutes. I flew through from one question to the next. I finished the test and stood up. Only ten minutes had passed.

"No way!" whispered a student.

When I handed Ma Baker the test, she smiled quizzically and said, "Really, Michael?"

I nodded and grinned back. I knew everything was okay.

Chapter 18: Silly

I received a B on that final and graduated with my A.A.S. in radiography. Next, I needed to take the national and California state exams to get my licenses. I had applied and was waiting to hear back about my test date and time.

Finally, the letter came. I was nervous and excited because I'd heard the test was so hard that a number of people didn't pass. When I ripped open the envelope and read the letter, my heart sank to my toes.

As an ex-felon on parole, you are ineligible to take the test.

It was as though an elephant sat down on my chest, squeezing every ounce of breath out of my lungs. What the hell was I going to do if I couldn't get licensed?

In the hopes there was something I could do, I talked to the school administration. They informed me that being an ex-felon was not the issue at hand; it was that I was still on parole. I had eighteen to twenty-four months left on parole. I was sunk.

I heard about a good attorney named William O'Mara and made

an appointment with him to see if he could help me in any way get licensed before I was off parole.

As he sat back in his big leather chair behind his big mahogany desk in his tiny office cluttered with papers, framed licenses, and degrees, I told my story.

"Well sir, it all started about five or six years ago, when I was set up and arrested for trafficking of a controlled substance by a NDI officer named John David Black."

"What did you say the officer's name was?" he asked.

"John David Black."

"Hmmm, that name sounds familiar."

"Well, sir, I did three years on a ten-year sentence in which I actually attended full time school. From there I completed another year of prerequisites and finally the radiography program at T.M.C.C. for x-ray."

"Great, good for you. So wherein lies the problem?"

I explained how I was told I couldn't take the test I needed to get my license to support myself, that my vocational training and income would end as soon as school was complete.

"I see this does pose a problem. I can probably help you out here, but it will cost around $2,500. There is no guarantee, though, you do understand?"

"Well, I have to at least try."

I finished filling out the paperwork and paid him so he could begin the process.

The next time we met, he told me something I never would have imagined in a million years.

"I have some information you might be interested in. I knew of John David Black; he has just been sentenced to a ten-year term in prison for trafficking steroids through the U.S. Mail."

What an incredible turn of events. John David Black was locked away, and I was a free man. Who would have thought this would be our destinies?

While waiting for a decision about my board exams, I took a job working as a laborer in the underground construction field. I was thirty years old. After all my schooling, being on the end of a shovel was not what I'd expected. Every day I shoveled and back-filled for eight to ten hours, picking up and moving large heavy PVC pipes used for sewer, water and electrical in new neighborhoods. The work was doable yet not enjoyable. There would be days when we were out in sub-zero weather, snow and ice, digging holes for the underground with a foot or two of water in some holes. Sometimes I would step into a hole, filling my Sorrel insulated work boots up with ice water. The insulated liner would get soaked, weighing an extra ten pounds as though filled with cement.

I got up at 4 a.m. to be at the gym by 4:30 then on the job site at 7 a.m. On the weekends and some weeknights I would bounce and or body guard for private strippers. My study materials gathered dust on the kitchen table. I wasn't that worried about it, though. I figured I'd have to wait the two years to take the exam. After six months or so of this construction work, I started to think, if I didn't get my x-ray license, I would go back to school for engineering. I now had the motivation to not do manual labor ever again.

When my workout out buddy and old roommate Chuck offered to get me on selling cars, I took it. We worked for a little lot in Reno with about ten other guys. And then I received the news: I had won the decision to be able to take the ARRT test and get certified. Both the judge and D.A. from Lovelock had written letters on my behalf to the court. All the praying, hoping and hard work I had poured into my education was paying off.

I pulled all the study material out of storage and had to relearn in ninety days everything I'd forgotten over the last year. This was no easy task; I knew people that flunked the ARRT right out of school. I began to wonder if I could actually do it. Luckily I had all my flash cards from each semester. I plowed through, a class and a semester at a time. The fact that Spring and a few of my friends were already working at some of the local hospitals kept me motivated. So did thinking about my time in prison; I figured if I could make it through that, I could do anything.

One day at work, a beautiful young woman and her husband walked on to the car lot. She had pretty green eyes like emeralds flashing as she blinked. Those eyes vibed happiness and kindness. She did not have a lick of make up on, yet she glowed like an angel. As I watched them walk around a bit, I could not take my eyes off her. I introduced myself, shaking their hands.

"Hi, I'm Celina, and this is my brother, Jose."

Her brother? It was my lucky day!

As we were test-driving Subarus she told me she needed room in her car for her chocolate lab; she liked to bring him along on hikes. She had just moved back home to Loyalton, a small one-horse town about 45 minutes from Reno. She had attended Evergreen College in Washington, where she'd studied to become a geologist. I was entranced. She was alluring, so unusual, beautiful, and smart.

I handed her my card and said, "If you'd like to have a nice dinner cooked for you, call me." She took the card and slid it in her purse, smiling.

"Thanks, Michael."

Lucky me, she called later that day.

"Hello, Michael, this is Celina, were you serious about dinner?"

"Very!"

We made a date for the next evening. I told her I would cook her dinner if she wanted to come over.

I lit candles and had nice music playing while I made my crushed red pepper, sun dried tomato pesto on penne pasta. We had an immediate connection, being drawn together as if it were meant to be. I learned that night she was almost ten years younger than me. This aided in my attraction to her. As we sat there drinking wine, laughing and staring into each other's eyes. I sang her a little song:

"Roses are red, violets are blue, who is the cutest little green-eyed Latina under the big blue sky? Little Chili Silly Pepper that's who." She leaned forward, gave me a generous kiss. The look in her eye said love.

"I want to be your little Silly Pepper forever!" she said.

From that time on her name was Silly Pepper. She loved it. She would always sign her love notes and cards:

"Love, Silly Pepper"

On testing day, I woke up nervous with knots in my stomach. I anticipated a four-hour test, but I was done in an hour and forty-five minutes. Really, that was it? I kept going over the test to make sure I had completed it. That couldn't be the whole test, I thought. It was way too easy. The next week I took the California boards, which took me all of ninety minutes to complete although we were allotted four hours. Once again I kept going over the test looking for more. Clearly, my teachers had prepared us well.

I was soon employed as an x-ray tech at one of the local hospitals, but I was consumed with the thoughts of going to Loma Linda University for the nuclear medicine program. I went through all the steps of filling out applications, getting letters of recommendation from Dr. Ghedny and Dr. Kullick, and writing a personal statement. I didn't know how I'd make it happen if I was accepted. I just knew I had to try, and with God's help it would work out.

I was then invited to interview at Loma Linda for the nuclear medicine program. I contacted Woody, who had gotten out of prison on parole and was living in Norco, which is located in between Loma Linda and Corona. He insisted I stayed with him the couple days I would be in town. I reached his home after an eight-hour drive and was tired, yet at the same time excited to see him.

"Well, Woodster," I said as we sat at his dining room table eating dinner, "Who would have thought six years ago you and I would be sitting here?"

"Brother, it feels good to be out here in the real world after all that shit we had to go through."

"It sure is a lot nicer sitting here looking back, then it was sitting in there looking ahead," I said.

"What a hell of a ride it has been. We just have to count our blessings, my brother. We both know what we do not want, that is back to prison. When I saw you come in and get through all that schooling and get your first parole, which was a wakeup call to me. I had spent nine years working in the dental lab making partials and other things for the dentist. I thought that would look good on my parole hearings. However, when I watched what you did, it made me think, maybe I should go to school too. And look at what that change did for me, I made my next parole."

"You did good, buddy. I'm proud of you. I am proud of both of us!"

Before bed that night Woody took me out to the garage and showed me the parts to his Pan-Head Harley that he was happily restoring. He was grinning from ear to ear, I could tell he was truly happy.

The next day when I got up and went to my interview, I was very nervous. I met with Art, the head of the nuclear medicine program.

"Michael," he said, "we consider this program equal to a post graduate in nuclear medicine."

"Really, that's even better, more bang for the buck," I replied.

"It takes either a bachelors in biology or to be licensed radiography through an accredited school. By the time you do all the prerequisites for the radiography courses and then the prerequisites for the nuclear medicine program you have the same course studies as a bachelors in biology and then some."

"Terrific, I am licensed radiography through TMCC, which is accredited through Loma Linda University. Not only that, I also have an A.A. in psychology."

"You're all set then."

We toured their nuclear medicine department. I was impressed at the size of their department, all their equipment and their radiopharmacy. When we shook hands, I was told they would be contacting me shortly with an answer. I returned to Reno the next day.

Silly called me one day and told me we needed to talk. I could tell by the tone of her voice she was very concerned. When she came over to the house, I prepared us dinner as usual. She looked me in the eye with those beautiful green eyes with little hazel specks. They seemed to be tearing up.

"I'm pregnant."

A tidal wave hit me.

Oh no, I thought. I knew I should have instead been thinking, *how wonderful.*

This couldn't happen right now. I'd just been accepted to Loma Linda. Having a kid would ruin everything I'd worked so hard for. Of course self-centered thinking was not what Silly was expecting to hear. I should have welcomed the fact with great joy and made arrangements for her to be with me through the schooling. Instead of thinking rationally, I started thinking desperately.

"Baby, we can't have this right now, it's the wrong time."

"I understand. I'm sorry to have let this happen," she said innocently, as tears ran down her cheeks.

My heart felt like it was being ripped out of my chest. I told her, "I promise if we can wait, we'll make a family when I'm finished with school."

"Promise?" she asked. "That's what I want with you."

"Yes sweetie, I promise." I told her. "When I get out of school, we will make a family."

"I love you," she said, drying her eyes.

"I love you too, Silly."

On the way to the clinic to get an abortion, we were both very quiet. When I dropped her off for the procedure, I almost turned back around to stop her. Yet something inside me wouldn't let me. Probably the biggest mistake in my life was made right then. It was one of the worst days of our lives. When I picked her up afterward, I could tell her heart was broken and my soul had withered. We tried to pretend everything was okay. But later that night neither one of us had an appetite at dinner. We cried in each other's arms.

Ten years ago, my friend from high school Joe and I had been consumed with talking about how to traffic half a pound of cocaine to Lovelock. And now we were talking about what I had to do to receive a postgraduate degree in Nuclear Medicine. He had just finished law school in Utah. I'd been accepted into the program but didn't know how I'd financially pull it off.

"After what you have been through, you'll never regret going," he said. "Do whatever it is you have to do to make this happen."

I decided to take out student loans and to get two semesters of very difficult prerequisites of chemistry and physics out of the way. I worked x-ray during the days and traveled 45 miles to Carson City for night classes. I also arranged to rent out my house when I left Reno for Southern California.

It was all coming together. I put in my two-week notice in at the hospital, and Silly and I had a nice vacation lined up to the California and Oregon Coast for two weeks. The last day I was at work, they were having a contest in radiology. A two-hundred-dollar dinner at one of the new restaurants in Reno to name Dr. Bruno's baby. His wife was in delivery and they had yet to decide on a name. Silly and I liked the name Michael Anthony. Before taking off for vacation, I slipped that name into the contest box.

Silly and I traveled the coast and stayed at various national campgrounds along the way. We could pull up and have our tent with queen-sized air mattress and camp set up like a home in about twenty minutes. We often had little competitions, making bets about who would finish the dishes first or who would find the next heart-shaped rock as we walked along the Yuba river. We visited the great red woods and would stop by the various tide pools scattered along the coast filled with quirky colorful creatures. We ended up in Brookings Oregon, at my grandfather's. He took us deep sea fishing and instead of learning about fishing, I learned about sea sickness, throwing up for six hours straight. I could think of nothing but getting back to stable land. In spite of it all, I caught thirteen cod. Bent over the edge of boat throwing up, I would see my pole bend. I mustered the energy to get up and reel it in. After re-baiting the hook and casting I'd haul myself over the side of the boat and continue chumming the fish.

When Silly and I returned to Reno and I went to get my last check, I discovered I had won the two-hundred-dollar dinner at Roxy Bistro's for naming Dr. Bruno's kid. I took Silly to dinner. Over candlelight and great music, we laughed and stared into each other's eyes. I always admired her beautiful green eyes with hazel specks. Silly was going to stay at her parents' in Loyalton, California. I'd be living with my old friend Martin in his house half an hour from Loma Linda. Silly and I had talked about how we would play it by ear. I told her she could date other people and if it was meant to be, then we'd be together later. It was very hard for me to say this; I did not want to lose her. Especially after what we had been through. However, I knew how a long-distance relationship could be. I didn't want things to be like they were with Betty. I knew it would break my heart if I continued to love her and she ended up leaving me. I had to be cold. I told her if we made it through this, we would marry and make the family that we should have already started.

Without her knowing I drove out to my sister's ranch to talk to my sister Lucy.

"Hey, do you still have grandma's wedding rings?"

"Yes, why do you ask?"

"I think, if we can make it through this next year, I'm going to ask Silly to marry me. But not till I know we will make it through Loma Linda. I do not want another Betty situation."

"Yes, I do have them, you can have them. I think that's a great idea. She loves you more than anyone ever loved you."

I would be heading to Southern California in a few days. I would ride my Harley down and have Silly follow me in my car. Then we would fly her back home.

Chapter 19: One Door Closes Another Opens

I was packed and ready to move when I received a phone call that would devastate me. Michelle, Big Dave's mother, told me in stricken voice that Dave's body was found at his ranch in the hay barn. It looked like suicide.

Dave always drank heavily. Even when he lived with me on I street, he would get up and have a six-pack for breakfast before leaving for work. I think he was trying to cope with what had happened years before, in high school on senior ditch day.

He and two of his best friends had been heading out to Pyramid Lake for the party. Dave was raised around racing and going fast. It was always in his blood. On the way to Pyramid Lake Dave was going way to fast, as usual, and passing dangerously. When he flew off the road, the car rolled over many times. That accident killed one of his best friends and put another in a wheelchair for life. I remember hearing my sisters talking about it when I was in junior high.

Although Big Dave said he drank to ease his back pain, perhaps drinking every day was the only way he could deal with the real pain, the pain of memory.

Suicide didn't make sense, though. Dave had just recently married, and they'd purchased a 40-acre ranch. He seemed genuinely happy. He was only 42 years old.

The funeral was very difficult for me. I knew almost everyone there like a second family. I just kept thinking to myself, *this was not how it's supposed to be, Big Dave*. I sat there in a daze, next to his parents and sister. Everyone we used to hang out with was there. There's John Valdez. Ed Anderson. People Big Dave lead as a guide on hunts.

As the pastor spoke, I didn't hear a word. I just bit back my tears and stared at Big Dave's artwork propped next to his casket. My eyes filled up with tears faster than I could push them down. Then it happened, I just let go. I was crying like a little baby for my old friend I would never see or talk to again. I still miss him to this day. I learned a great deal from Dave. In fact, Dave influenced my art that has sold very well for the past few years. I often thought about him as I was working on this line of art, wishing he were here. I know he would have been excited about it. RIP, my friend.

The next couple days seemed surreal. I was off to study in nuclear medicine at a major medical university. Yet Dave's death shadowed my departure to Southern California.

Finally, I was on my Harley, the wind in my face heading south, with Silly following close behind in my car. As I journeyed farther from Reno and closer to Southern California, I felt the promise of a new beginning build in my bones. I passed the place along the highway where Danny and I stayed for the day on the drilling rig fourteen years ago. Shortly after that, I passed Four Corners, where I lost the use of my right hand in a fight with Big Dave's little brother. As I passed Woody's mom's old house on the way to Martins, I knew I was only thirty minutes away from Corona. My past. The culmination of my life. How I had made it this far? I had no idea. It felt at that moment like everything was flowing, as it should, as though I was in sync with God's guidance.

After an eight-hour ride and through a few dust and smog storms we made it to Martin's house. Martin was a little shorter than I was and always in very good shape, dark hair framing his smiling face. We'd met years ago when I did hair down in Costa Mesa. We'd hang out, party and smoke weed. His wife, Lita, was so beautiful; I would admire her from afar. I moved in with them right before I left Southern California to return to Reno.

Martin's sister Carrie was also gorgeous, and I'd had a crush on her. One night, all those years before, we were both staying in the living room trying to sleep on the couches. She'd just had a fight with her husband. Somehow we ended up lying next to each other, and she was telling me how much she liked me and I was telling her how attracted I was to her. As we talked I craved touching her sweet curves and thick brown hair.

All the talking was hot foreplay. Soon we were in each other's arms, rolling around the living room floor. We agreed to keep our night of passion to ourselves.

A few weeks later, I came home from work to meet up with Lita; she and I were supposed to join Martin at the sushi bar for dinner. As I was getting ready to shower, Lita approached me.

"Cliff, can I join you in your shower?" she asked.

"What?" Had I heard her correctly?

"Come on let me join you in the shower, it will be fun!"

Imagining her naked, it was all I could do to say, "No, I can't do that to Martin." Even though I'd only known Martin a few months, I really liked the guy. I would never be able to look myself in the mirror again let alone Martin in the eyes.

"Oh come on," she said. "Carrie told me what you guys did the other night. She said you were the best lover she'd ever had."

"Believe me, Lita," I said, making sure the towel was wrapped tightly around my waist. "If you weren't with Martin, I'd be all over you."

"I understand, Cliff," she said. Turning to open the door. "You're a good friend."

"Thank you, Lita. Let's not mention this again."

That night at sushi, Lita said to Martin, "You and Cliff will be friends forever."

Years later, after the accident with my right hand and the fuel pump, I was visiting them. One day while Martin was at work, Lita and I were watching TV on the couch. A commercial for Lipton Tea came on showing a woman diving into a pool and swimming under water to other side. When she comes up she kisses a man at the other end of the pool.

"I sure wish someone would kiss me like that." Lita said.

"Oh, I'm sure Martin kisses you like that often," I replied.

"No he doesn't. I want that kind of passion with someone."

I got uncomfortable, realizing this gorgeous woman, the wife of my good friend, was once again coming on to me. It took all the discipline in every bone of my body to get up off that couch.

While I was in prison, Martin caught her having an affair. They were soon divorced.

Martin was now living in the four-bedroom two-bath house alone and in perfect location for me to go to Loma Linda. I would be his roommate. Everything fell into place as if the Good Lord wanted it to happen this way.

And yet I knew I had to say goodbye to Silly. I wasn't sure what was to come. But I felt as though part of me was about to be removed.

I felt a void.

We had a beautiful weekend together riding the Harley down to the 101 alongside the ocean, the salt air in our faces and the warm inviting sun on our backs. We rode down to Laguna, San Juan Capistrano, Dana Point and San Clemente, where my aunt and uncle live. From there we cut through the Ortega Highway past Lake Elsinore then down the 215 to Temecula then up the 76 to Mount Palomar through the orchards, inhaling the intoxicating fragrance of orange blossoms. Truly, one of the happiest moments of my life.

Chapter 20: Loma Linda

The university was its own neighborhood. The bookstore down one street, the hospital a couple blocks over. Restaurants, activities centers, theaters. You name it; it was there. I was amazed at the vastness. God had blessed me well.

I had my routine down in a week or two. The first semester, I started my week with physics class at Loma Linda Hospital, a 900-bed facility. It felt like if you got lost in the vast hallways, you wouldn't be found for days. The other four days, I did clinical at various hospitals.

My instructors at Parkview Hospital in Riverside were a young guy named Ed and an older lady named Marlene. They both had great senses of humor, which made working in the small eighty-bed hospital fun.

The first day, Ed asked me, "With those hands, have you ever tried to start an IV?"

"No, never. I was hoping I could learn how."

"It's crucial to learn. We have to do our own IVs and you have to be very skilled at it. Our patients are very sick and a lot of them have been on chemo, which makes the veins very fragile. It's usually one of us in nuclear medicine that are called into the ER to get a vein when the emergency nurse can't."

"I didn't take out $20,000 in student loans and reroute my life to fail. If there is a way, I will learn it."

At Parkview, I met Paul, who would transport our patient's pre and post exams. With pearly skin so light it was almost translucent, a swish to his walk, bent wrist and a hilarious way with his words, he reminded me of some of the gay guys I had worked with in my hair styling days. Ed, knowing Paul liked me, asked Paul if I could learn IVs on him.

"In other words," Ed said, "you may get poked a few times."

We all laughed.

"Well you certainly know, I would let this guy poke me anytime," Paul said flirtatiously.

Ed watched closely as I nervously tried sticking Paul in the anterior elbow. I went slowly at first, but could tell this caused a lot of pain as it seemed the needle hesitated to pierce the skin. I could tell by the look on Paul's face he was not enjoying it. I had to give him credit; I wouldn't let anyone practice on me. I started to sweat. I had blood from one end of me to the other trying to use a regular IV. I just did not have the dexterity with my right hand to twist the cap on the IV after pulling the needle out. Then Ed figured out I needed a special IV called a safety-intima. With a safety-intima, you'd pull out the stylet (or needle), leaving just a flexible plastic tube left in the patient to inject through. It was a closed system so I did not have to screw a cap on to stop the blood from coming out. Ed explained to me that if I stretched the skin tight as if to give a tattoo, the needle would pierce the skin much easier. I got it down in a few tries. Paul was amazed at how painless it was once I stretched the skin tightly.

At every hospital where I introduce the safety-intima, the nurses thanked me because they were so simple and quick to use. Years later, I was inserting an IV into a patient, at the prestigious Cardiology Consultants of Napa Valley. When I told the patient I had inserted the IV and administered the radiopharmaceutical for heart imaging, she looked at me and said, "No way! I teach phlebotomy at the hospital next door. That was not only the best but the most pain-free IV I have ever had."

Laughing, I showed her my hands. "And I did that with these."

She asked me if I would come to her class to show her students my hands. She said, "They all cry about how hard it was to insert an IV. I would love to introduce you to them and show them the hands you have to work with and the job you do."

"No problem, it would be my pleasure," I happily said.

After clinical or class, I would go to the gym down the street from Martin's house. I figured I could hit it every night on the way home. The day I joined the gym a super-fit women wearing a tiny mini skirt and pumps helped me get registered. Debbie was a professional body builder; it was very difficult for me to keep my eyes off her amazing body. She had long blond hair and beautiful hazel eyes with a great smile showing off her luscious mouth. After I left the gym that day I headed straight for a pay phone down the street. I called the gym and asked to speak with her.

"Hello, this is Debbie."

"Hello, this is Michael, you just helped my register for your gym."

"The big guy with blue eyes?" she asked.

"Yes, that'd be me."

"How can I help you, handsome?"

"I was just wondering if you were single and would like to go out sometime?" I boldly asked.

"I would love to."

"How about dinner at T.B. Scotts tonight?"

Without hesitation, she answered, "Sounds great to me, what time?"

While sitting in the dining room surrounded by salt-water fish tanks teeming with brightly colored fish, I marveled at her body. Her skin was tan and silky smooth; her quads were big and powerful, very sexy to me.

"Guess it's my lucky day," I said. "I am sure you get asked out constantly at the gym."

"Not really, I seem to intimidate most men," she said. "I'm glad you had the balls to ask me out."

"Me too," I replied with a huge smile on my face.

After a nice dinner, I walked her to her car. I wanted to touch her, feel her, beautiful hard, tan body. We dove into a long wet kiss. I liked everything, but I thought I felt razor stubble around her mouth. What the heck? I went home that night I was wondering why she felt that way when I kissed her. I invited her over the next night to make her dinner. After dinner we started to make out again. I felt the razor stubble again. By now we had finished dinner and were laying on my bed in my room.

"Do you shave your face, baby?" I asked.

"Yes, I'm sorry did you feel stubble?"

"Yes, I thought so the first time we kissed, too."

I had read that if a woman is taking steroids it can enlarge a woman's clit and give her facial hair. Not only that she can become very sexual. I prayed that was true for her!

As she started to undo her blouse, I could see she was wearing a sexy pink bra. And under that she had a very tight tortoise shell stomach and firm fake boobs. Then she started to un button her pants. I helped her pull them off for they were very tight and difficult to pull over her perfect apple-shaped ass. She lay there in here pink panties and matching bra with the most beautiful body I had ever laid eyes on. I was so aroused, almost drooling. She asked if I liked what I saw.

"Yes, very much," I said.

"I have taken steroids to get this body and be able to compete," she explained. "That causes me to have facial hair so I have to shave. I hope you don't mind."

"As long as you're all woman." I replied.

As she slid her panties down, I indeed saw that her clitoris was enlarged and swollen. We started in like animals in heat, having marathon sex all night long. She was pure passion waiting to be taken. And take her I did.

She was a few years older than me and when we did go out, we always had fun. When we rode the Harley down to the beach if she wore a mini skirt on the bike, every guy driving by would honk and wave. Though we had more passion than I had ever experienced, deep down I knew she could never replace Silly. Debbie had a daughter and already made a family with someone else. The very thing I wanted with Silly. I was also craving Silly's youth and innocence compared to Debbie's maturity. There was something about Silly being so much younger than myself that I really enjoyed. When she was around, I felt much younger at heart. I had to end my relationship with Debbie before it really ever started. Yet we remained great friends.

A few semesters into my program, I had to start my internships out in Palm Springs, a two hour commute each way. By the time I would get to the gym it would be seven p.m., so I wouldn't get home until nine or nine-thirty. I had to leave for clinic in Palm Springs at five thirty in the morning and spend the weekends studying. By the time I got in bed after the gym, I would be so exhausted yet my metabolism would be so amped up from my workout and the gym, I couldn't fall asleep until two or three in the morning. When I had trouble staying awake on my drive to Palm Springs, I had to make a decision: either die falling asleep at the wheel or quit body building. I had to put my education first, yet it was depressing to watch my great shape deteriorate.

I decided I'd better concentrate on my schooling and hit the gym when I had time or days off. Once again I was achieving a 3.85 GPA and better. And once again, I was one of the first ones to hand my tests in.

Although I was enjoying the field of nuclear medicine, I was getting burnt out on studying. I had been doing it for seven years straight, summers included. It was getting difficult to sit at the table with my head buried in the books. I could only sit there maybe twenty to thirty minutes at a time, then I had to get up and take a break. I was getting headaches constantly. I had tossed around in my head the idea of going to a Physicians-Assistant school after Loma Linda, which would have taken me another two years. I just could not motivate myself for that.

One Valentine's Day weekend Silly came to see me. I always loved it when she came to visit. It was a delight to have her near me. But I did not show my feelings well; it was hard for me to be mushy and soft. I had spent so many years trying to harden myself, molding my behavior so as not to be malleable by other people. I would think about nice things she might like to hear; yet when I would try to communicate these things, the words would just stick in my throat. I did love her very much and knew we would make a great family with similar values and goals. I knew our children would grow up to be smart, beautiful and athletic. We talked often how we would raise our kids; education and sports were always a big part of our plans. We believed a busy child is a happy child. I wanted to be the football or wrestling coach with my children playing for the team. Or the dad that brings his kids to the gym to learn to live a healthy lifestyle.

Silly and I had a wonderful time, going out to nice dinners and taking romantic rides down the PCH on the Harley for the week. We also enjoyed cooking our own romance at home. We had great culinary skills and would put on good music. Louis Prima and Keely Smith made a great team; we loved to listen to their album while heating things up in the kitchen. Health conscious, we cooked very clean, all fresh vegetables and lean meats. One evening while I was cooking my chicken piccatta, Silly was at the sink washing dishes. She was wearing a little beige mini skirt with a tight white body shirt, I was noticing how tan and smooth her legs and arms were. As I walked up behind her, I put my arms around her waist and started to kiss the back of her neck. Then I nibbled my way around to her tiny ear, turning her, pulling her in close to kiss her forehead. Finally planting a long kiss on her lips.

"Silly Pepper, you know I love you very much."

"I think I do, I hope so, I love you too," she replied. "In fact I don't think you know how much I love you Cliff." I actually came here this weekend to break up with you. I heard through the grapevine that you had been dating some body builder woman. This broke my heart, Cliff."

"What?" I asked, "Who told you this?"

"One of your work out buddies," she said. "Then he asked me out."

"Silly, I did meet a woman at the gym." I knew I had to admit it but I couldn't tell her the whole truth. She would leave me. *God, what had I done?* "We had dinner a couple of times. Although when I was with her, I would think of you, and how much I love you. It was because of this that I know I love you more than anything or anyone in my life." I realized I needed to make sure she knew I wasn't really cheating. "Remember I said before I left we could see other people?"

"I didn't want that. You are the one I want to be with. I love you!"

"How much, baby?"

"More than I have ever loved anyone," she said. "In fact I wish you were the first one I had ever been with."

I kneeled to one knee, pulling the ring out of my pocket I had secretly gone to my room to gather. I'd wanted to do this at a restaurant or public place. But it felt like the right moment, very touching and sincere.

"Will you marry me, Silly?"

"Yes. Yes I will marry you, Cliff."

The gleam in her green eyes was of pure elation as I slowly slid the ring on to her finger. We kissed and held each other tightly.

When it was time for her to leave, as she drove away to head back home. I prayed to God for her to have a safe trip, to please never let anything happen to her. Finally, I'd found the one I wanted to spend the rest of my life with.

Coming from as low as a man can go, to as high as one can achieve, made me feel like I was on top of the world. Finals were near. Only six weeks out, and I had filed for the California and national boards. In my photo album I had a picture of me posing in Carson Prison only six years previously. Now I had a picture of me with my fellow post-graduates in nuclear medicine.

One day, with the excitement of graduation filling me, I was pulling blood from a patient with AIDS in preparation for a MUGA, a multigated study of the heart to view it in motion. This tells us how hard the heart is contracting and in return how much volume of blood it is moving through. It's a common study, but not always common to be pulling HIV blood. Once I pull about 10 ml of the patient's blood I tag it with a radioactive material called TC04, Technisium Pertecnatate. After drawing the blood from the patient, I went into the Hot Lab to transfer the blood to a small vile to tag it. The Hot Lab is the area designated to Nuclear Personal only, an area where we store, prepare and mix radioactive materials. It has lead-lined walls and an area with lead bricks that we work behind, keeping the radiation at bay. I was pulling the labeled blood from the vial with a syringe and 18-gage needle attached, to re-administer it to the patient. And then it happened. I accidentally poked myself with the contaminated needle.

I felt the sharp pierce into my right hand at the base of my thumb.

Frantically, yet not wanting the patient to know what had just happened, I set the vial and the syringe down at the work station behind the lead bricks. This right here, is a medical personnel's worse night mare. You only pray to God this never happens to you. I felt my heart collapse. My stomach shot into my mouth. Thoughts came screaming into my head: I was going to die. I just killed myself. Was this really how I was going to die, after all I'd been through? How was I going to explain this to Silly?

Nervously I scurried up to John, the manager, and explained what had just happened. John's face turned ghost white,

"Oh shit. Come on. We have to get you to emergency now."

We rushed through the hallways to ER. John explained to the nurse working, what had just happened. She frowned. A bad sign. Placing me in a private room she told me to be patient and calm down, the doctor would be right in. As I was sitting there almost in tears. I noticed a graph above the door starting at one and going to 1,000,000,000, I wondered what it was.

When the doctor walked in, I said, "I think I just killed myself."

"Explain to me exactly what happened," he said.

I did, my voice quavering.

"Were you wearing gloves?" he asked. "Please tell me you were."

"Yes sir, I was," I frantically said.

"Show me where you stuck yourself."

I showed him the little red mark at the base of my thumb on my right hand.

He examined it then calmly walked over to the door and pointed up to the graph.

This must be the "I am stupid enough to poke myself with an HIV contaminated needle" room, I thought.

"It's very fortunate you were wearing gloves," he said. "Any contamination probably wiped off on the glove material before it entered your skin. Not only that, but it takes a puncture to the vein directly to introduce enough of the virus to be concerned. It doesn't look like the needle made it that far."

I started to feel a little relief. Yet I know no one in the medical field can guarantee you a 100% prognosis.

"Yes, there's a little room for concern," he continued. Once again, I felt my heart collapse. "No one really ever knows."

He pointed to the graph above the door with a long stick with a black rubber end. There was a little red mark amongst the black lines in the graph. The red mark was at the left end of the 1,000,000,000 graph, not at the 0 end. He told me I had about a one in a billion chance of contracting the HIV from the incident.

One in a billion. I thought about my life, about the drilling rig accident, the fuel pump accident and glasses off the dead body my brother-in-law had given me. It would be just like me to be that one in a billion.

"We'd better put you on PEP, Post-exposure Prophylaxis or antiretroviral medication drugs to kill the virus just in case," he said.

Just in case.

The PEP meds made me nauseous, achy, and weak like I had a bad flu. I could barely sit up, let alone walk. Only two weeks to graduation, I was so sick I didn't think I could pull off my finals and the last of the clinical. Maybe this was one last test from God to see how dedicated I really was.

I decided to fly to Sacramento to tell Silly in person what had happened. As I was on the 90-minute flight, I knew I had to tell her and give her the option to leave me, so she would not have to deal with this drama and stress. I was very scared. As I sat there next to a good looking woman, she started a conversation and wanted to know what I was going to be doing in Sacramento.

"Hi I'm Sally. How are you doing today?"

I didn't really feel like talking to her. But I remained professional.

"Cliff. My pleasure."

"I just love Sacramento, don't you?" she asked.

"Yes, it's a very pretty place, a little hot though," I replied.

"How long are you here for?" she asked just as the plane was setting down on the runway.

"Just flying in for the weekend, and you?"

"Oh I live here, just returning from Riverside." she explained. "What do you do?"

"I'm just graduating Loma Linda University for Nuclear medicine," I explained.

"Well," she said, handing me a card, "if you need a place to stay or someone to hang with, here's my number."

Surprised, I took the number out of my hand and handed it back to her.

"Thank you, but I don't think my fiancé would understand." I smiled.

"Lucky girl," she replied.

Silly was waiting there at the gate for me, wearing a little brown summer dress and her open-toed sandals revealing pedicured toes. As soon as I looked at her beautiful green eyes, I started to choke up.

"Hello sweetie, how are you?" she asked.

"I'm okay. Let's get out of here and get home." I felt as though I was going to vomit.

As she was driving us home in her little silver Subaru, I started to explain what had happened.

"Silly, there's something I have to tell you," I said nervously.

"What is it, Cliff?" she asked. "Are you alright?"

"Baby, I have to tell you something very important. Last week, I poked myself with an HIV-contaminated needle."

I could see the tears building in her eyes.

"What do you mean?" she asked.

"I accidentally poked myself with a needle while working on an HIV patient," I said. "You need to know this, the doctor said there is a one in a billion chance that I will contract HIV. I had gloves on and it was not a very deep poke. I will probably not get HIV. However, they have put me on some very strong drugs to help prevent HIV. I am very sick to my stomach and don't feel well at all right now from these drugs. I was so sick last week I missed a couple classes. I'm not sure if I can continue and finish the program."

"Oh God." She had a blank look on her face, like she'd gone numb.

"You need to decide whether you want to continue to be with me. I understand if you don't."

A minute of silence seemed like a day.

"Cliff, if I left you, I would spend the rest of my life looking for someone just like you."

We spent that evening having a bowl of soup at a little Asian restaurant down the street. That was all I could stomach.

We spent the rest of the weekend talking and dreaming about all the things we were going to finally get to do. About our future and how it would be worth the wait.

Finally, I graduated Loma Linda with honors. A couple weeks after that I finished the PEP medication for the HIV. I had to have a HIV tests done every other month for a few months, then at six months and then a year later. Every couple of years I needed to be checked to make sure I didn't contract it. I started to feel much better, back to normal once the meds stopped. After another thirty days of studying at the kitchen table, I passed my four-hour boards as well in only two hours. It was surreal that I had gone from prison to this.

And now, my seven years of schooling all that studying, all those months including summers were over. A permanent smile was affixed to my face for months.

My field was in demand. Many hospitals were offering $10,000 sign-on bonuses for nuclear medicine personnel. I could have a job anywhere I wanted.

"I'll go anywhere you want, Silly. Name it."

She chose Sacramento, because she was going to change careers and study at Sacramento City College to be a dental hygienist.

When Mercy San Juan Hospital in Sacramento offered me a job, I sold my house in Sparks to start a new life in Sacramento with Silly Pepper.

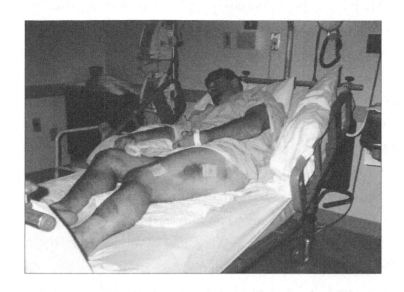

Chapter 21: Crash

Silly and I were planning to move in with her sister Anette into her two-bedroom apartment. Anette was going to buy a house soon, and the apartment would be ours. It was small but we loved the place. It sat back off the street and was somewhat private, located in a lovely older section of the city with tree-lined streets and yards resembling a painter's pallet laden with colorful perennial flowers and fruit trees. In the mornings Silly and I would jog a mile down to the zoo and back. As we jogged we could reach out to fruit trees and snag an orange or persimmons.

On cold days, we jogged after work and then stopped at a quaint Chinese restaurant for a hot bowl of wor wonton soup. Just thinking about it made us hungry and we ran a little faster to finish our workout. Flounder, sea bass, shrimp and crab floated in the tanks at the rear of the restaurant, whose tables were covered in white tablecloths. The family-owned place was so cozy and inviting and always filled with Asian diners, so we knew it must be good.

My job was busy and fast-paced. I was working with two nuclear physicians and six full-time techs like myself. The ER had 32 beds, filled to capacity most days.

Usually I'd get called in at 7 p.m. and work a couple hours. Then I'd go home and often get called in again around 1 or 2 a.m., which usually led to being there all night. Sometimes on my thirty-minute drive to the hospital, I'd start to nod off and have to shake myself awake.

I was very tired after work from all the new stress. Sometimes Silly would want to talk to me late at night. I'd be nearly asleep, and she would nudge me, asking me to pull my earplugs.

I got mad at her for waking me. "We can talk about it in the morning," I'd say. But we never did.

One night when I got home from work, Silly was nowhere to be found. There was a note by the bed in Silly's handwriting saying that a woman from Southern California had called. Someone I used to date. She wanted me to call her back.

I'm at my sisters Denise's house, said the note. *I am going to stay here for a while because you lied to me.*

"Silly, what's going on?" I asked her on the phone.

"Who is that woman that called?"

"I told you I had dated the body builder a couple times. Was that her?" I asked.

"I don't know who it was."

"Well Silly, we have already discussed this, and I thought we resolved it, I'm sorry she called. But don't worry, please. I am here with you, am I not?"

"I was making us a nice dinner when she called. It made me so mad, I just packed a few things and figured I would come out here and stay a few days."

"Please come home, I miss you and do not want to fight with you."

"Let me think about it Cliff."

She finally came home later that night and we kissed and made up. However, I was left with an uneasy feeling. Why was she so insecure?

With Anette working nights, Silly and I needed to be very quiet when we would get home from work. We often hung out in our room so her sister could sleep. Not only did we have to stay in a small room but we had to whisper so as not to upset her sister. I wasn't prepared to live this way. Three years in prison was more than enough stressful communal living. I felt like a little kid not wanting to wake his parents, fearing the wrath that would come if I did. Anette's plan to buy a house had been postponed, so who knew how long we'd have to live this way?

I had taken the money from the sale of my house and put it into a 30-foot offshore racing boat. It was long and sleek like a cigarette boat on Miami Vice. Bright orange and with duel blown 501 Chevy motors, it would do over one hundred miles per hour on Tahoe. I still had the need for speed in my bones. I had always owned boats, and fell in love with this one as soon as we test-drove it. On the lake, I opened it up, and the G-force glued Silly into the back seat. She was pinned in like a bug stuck to the windshield. I could see in her eyes, she was excited. The blowers were so loud they sounded like a woman sitting on the engine cover screaming at the top of her lungs. This increased my adrenaline even more. I figured I would leave the money tied up in the boat, so I would not piddle it way. When we found a home we liked I could just sell the boat and get my money back.

But now I knew I should have invested the money into another house so we wouldn't be in this situation. The stressful living circumstances along with her insecurities led us to fight a lot. Perhaps, I suggested, it would be best if I looked for my own place. When I mentioned this, I could tell she was not happy. When I looked into her eyes I melted, I decided against moving out on my own. I was hoping we could mend our differences. I still knew she was the only woman for me.

Not only did I have call at Mercy San Juan, but on occasion, the techs at Mercy San Juan had to cover call for Mercy Folsom. Mercy Folsom only had one tech. When he went on vacation the doctors would ask us to cover for him. One night after call I had gotten home around 1 a.m. and crawled into bed and went to snuggle up to Silly. Spooning was our favorite snuggle position. She was cold and stiff, not receptive as usual.

"Where were you?" she asked.

"What do you mean, where was I?"

"You weren't at the hospital!"

"What, where was I then?" I asked again.

"Probably out with some blond with big boobs!"

She was always insecure about my past as a bouncer and body guard for strippers.

"What the hell are you talking about?"

"I called the hospital, they said you weren't there."

"Which hospital did you call?" I asked, getting short on patience.

"What do you mean, what hospital? The one where you work."

"Well there Einstein, I was at Mercy Folsom this time."

"No you weren't, you were probably out with some girl!"

I couldn't convince her otherwise. She rolled over, away from me, refusing to talk anymore.

Within a week or two of this incident, one of the female radiologists approached me in the reading room, where the doctors sit to read radiology films.

"I got a strange call from a woman who said you were her boyfriend. She told me to keep my distance."

I flushed with embarrassment. This was my work colleague. I had her number so I could call her quickly to view the films I had just sent her.

That night at dinner, I said to Silly, "Did you go through my phone and call someone?

nymore." I c

back. Ma   and left a
                              mess

he cried, the n.

felt stuck. I want   tors."

drove, or walked or   you.

me from doing it.

'd just wanted to lash out a.

hrobbing.

rents was silent. I felt my hear

ibal Lector's mask and could not

ext door was vacant, I approached

rrangement. I repainted the entire

as though Silly and I were starting

created a little garden area in the

he fence out back, and Silly made

ter getting up at 4:30 a.m. to go to

fast while she packed our lunches

be we were getting over our issues.

ew house, I went to a motorcycle

where I'd heard there were good

st three years, I'd been riding n

m bike, with the fairing, har

aint with billet wheels

t any mechanic th   er

t style brakes   . An
                         irra   t her.
reat grip
e mos   knew I   s said, I
                                 ny mouth.
Dyna W.

"I'm not even attracted to you a
made you ugly to me. I want the ring
day at a time."

She started to cry. The more
I wanted to apologize but my tongu
grab her hand like I usually did as w
the grocery store. Yet something kep

I didn't mean what I had said.
gripped the steering wheel, my head

The rest of the way to my p
breaking, but it was if I wore Han
speak.

When we noticed the home r
the owners and made a rent-to-own
place wanting, a fresh start. It seemed
to get back into the groove. She ha
yard. Blackberry vines crawled over
turnovers with the delicious fruit. A
the gym together, I'd cook us break
before we left for work. It seemed ma

Soon after moving into our r
shop down the street from my worl
deals on some nice bikes. For the l
Harley FLH. It was a beautiful custc
stereo, windshield and custom pearl
brakes. The brakes were so touchy th
almost end it. However, I needed th
my right hand since I didn't have a
FLH meant Full Luxury Hog. It is t
make. Yet, all my friends were ridin

and other fast bikes that had no fairings, no bags no stereos. Tired of bringing up the rear, I yearned for a faster bike. At the shop I found one: A Harley, Bad Boy, like Fat Boy, a soft tail but it had the springer front end. Nice black on blue paint. I had them add a Thunderheader exhaust, custom billet pegs and many more extras.

When I got home, Silly was pissed I had traded my bike in. She thought she should have been consulted for the transaction. I had figured it was my bike, my deal.

A few weeks later, Kathy from my bank called me. I really liked her. She had helped with the mortgage on my house. An old friend, she and I had spent time on Tahoe with our boats. "Michael," she said. "I do not know about the women you pick." She laughed.

"What do you mean?"

"Remember your girlfriend Cindy didn't like me? And now I received a phone message from your new girl telling me you are hers and for me to keep away."

Oh no, not her too? I thought Silly had lain off this weird possessive behavior.

"I'm sorry, Kathy," I said. "She's young and I guess insecure."

"No biggie, I understand. Maybe one day she will grow up." She laughed again.

"Let's hope she does it soon," I replied.

I was furious. When I approached Silly, she said I needed to show her and tell her more that I loved her. Maybe so. But her behavior turned me off. It was hard to tell her I loved her when she was acting so immature. I thought, maybe she needed someone younger, and I needed someone older. In fact, when she told me she wanted me to do something differently I'd say, "If you don't like it, don't let the door hit you in the ass on the way out." Maybe she wasn't the only one who needed to grow up.

Other times the words "I love you so much" or "I am so glad to be with you, I never want to lose you," would hover on the tip of my tongue. But for some reason they'd get stuck in my throat. I would just smile, thinking she must already know.

In July Silly's best friend from childhood was to be married. Silly was all excited and of course we were both attending. But I was still mad about calls she'd made to the people on my phone. I decided I'd go to Reno instead.

"Really, so you want me to go alone to my best friend's wedding?" she said.

"After what you've done, you sure can. I really don't care to go or see your friends."

"What are you going to do in Reno?"

"I don't know yet, I just know I am not going with you to that wedding."

"Well that kind of sucks, don't you think?"

"Oh, I'm sure you'll be just fine."

She moped around the house for the next few days. Every time she would walk by me or pass me in the hallway she'd either utter something under her breath or just give out an annoying sigh. Whenever I asked her what she said, she would get annoyed and tell me to never mind.

When the weekend of the wedding came, I fled on my new bike over the hill to Reno. It was a relief to escape the drama. As I was flying down the highway, I enjoyed its speed its responsiveness and the ride of the springer front end. Much more of a thrill to ride than the FLH. But I did not like the awkwardness of the way it cornered with the new handlebars. I was not used to my body catching all the wind without the fairing and windshield. I also missed my old brakes; this bike had stock brakes and took me nearly one hundred yards to come to a stop doing my usual speed of 80 miles per hour. The old bike would stop in less than half that distance.

By the time I reached Reno, my hands were tired and sore from hanging on to the ape hangers in the wind. The handlebars sat high in the air, the level of my shoulders. This caused my hands to go numb due to a previous neck injury in Judo. What a mistake I thought. I consoled myself with the fact that I liked the speed of the new bike.

I met up with Chance and Robert and a few of their friends. We started by hitting our old stomping grounds, Ed's Fantasy Girls, a strip bar where a lot of my buddies worked. As usual we got in for free. It's nice having friends at the door. And not paying for drinks, as they were handed to us by familiar faces from behind the bar. It had been a while since I'd seen the place, the soft pink and blue neon lights glowing in the background, loud music throbbing through the air and naked girls on stages everywhere. A few of the girls I knew came up and said hi, asked how I was doing. It didn't take long to get a few drinks down them. We shared a mind-eraser or two, a very strong drink with multiple straws, everyone competing to finish the drink. With the warming, numbing feelings of alcohol mixing in my blood, I was immediately in a better mood. It was just like old times, only now my pockets were full of cash from a great job. Most the girls who knew me knew I wasn't there for couch dances. Only the eye candy. You got more respect that way because they knew they couldn't play you. Hanging around pounding down the Jack Daniels like ice-cold water on a hot summer day, soon we were laughing and joking and tearing each other up. Once we'd made our rounds flirting with girls, it was time for the next stop. The Mustang Ranch Brothel was rumored to have been taken over by an infamous one-percenter motorcycle group.

Normally the brothel was about a thirty-minute ride from Ed's. But feeling no pain, the alcohol and adrenaline racing through our veins, the race was on. No fear for the law, we'd head out balls to the wall. Throttles wide open, motors screaming for mercy. No one wants to be the pussy in the rear. I flew down the highway, wind-tears flowing from behind my glasses. We made it in fifteen minutes, lucky no one died on the way.

There was no being foolish at the brothel or the one-percenters would have your ass. Yet it was where the bad boys hung out and the women were as naughty as they come. Old Bridge was a little old house with aged red and gold crushed velvet wallpaper. Old Rock: Van Morrison, The Doors, Janis Joplin played on the jukebox in the corner of the main lobby. A few old claw-legged leather chairs usually comforted a passed-out customer or biker. Well-worn red carpet led the way to the bar, where Donnie mixed drinks like a chemist. He knew what we liked and pulled the Jack off the shelf, setting it on the bar. We would buy a bottle at a time. The cigarette smoke was so thick you could cut it with a knife; it would burn your eyes and throat. Girls in nothing more than a G-string or a see-through nighty paraded around the room rubbing up against you trying to get you excited. I wasn't planning to cheat on Silly. This was just a place we liked to hang. In fact, while I was sitting there with my friends drinking and busting each others' chops, I was missing Silly. I realized I had made a mistake not going to the wedding with her. *What a Fucking idiot I am*, I kept thinking. At four a.m. we could barley walk. Slurring our words, it was a nice time to scream down the highway at 120 MPR to a casino for breakfast.

When I got home, I hugged Silly. But she stayed cold and rigid. I tried to warm her back up by saying, "I'm sure glad I'm here with you. If I still lived in Reno, I would probably have a DUI in no time hanging out with my friends."

But it was the silent treatment for me. In the next few days, she continued her little uttering under her breath every time she passed me. One day I noticed she was sitting out on the back porch, circling ads for room rentals.

"What are you doing?" I asked.

"What does it matter?" she asked.

"You're right, I guess it doesn't anymore," I replied.

I was sad to see where we were at that moment. After all the good times we had and all the promises we made for the future, I should have never canceled the trip to her friend's wedding.

"Do you want a ride to True Value to get some plants for your garden?" I asked.

"No, maybe some other time."

The phone rang, I picked it up. A guy asked for Celina.

"Excuse me, who is this?" I asked.

"You can tell her, it's Jason." Attitude.

"Does she know you?" My blood was starting to boil.

"Sure does!"

Obviously, the dude wasn't going to give an inch.

"Hey, phone's for you," I said to Silly. "You can tell this guy if he wants to continue his attitude, he's headed for an ass whipping." I hoped he would hear me.

Silly just rolled her eyes and took the phone, talking sweetly into it. "Oh hey, how are you doing? It sure was nice to see you too."

I couldn't listen to this crap. I went into the kitchen to make some tea. I couldn't hear her words, but her tone made it clear she was enjoying talking to this guy. When she got off the phone I asked, "Who was that?"

"Jason." An old high school friend I saw at the wedding."

"Well, you can tell Jason, if he wants to have an attitude with me, he can come on over here and have one to my face. I'll knock his fucking ass out!"

Silly turned and left the room.

Silly applied online for a job as a geologist with USGS and was hired. She had to leave for San Diego for a week of training. She seemed eager to start her new career. As we lay in bed the morning I was to take her to the airport to fly out, we were spooning, holding each other tightly,

"You know Cliff, this is my favorite part of the day, lying here in bed with you."

"Mine too sweetie," I said. "I do love you with all my might." Sometimes I could say it. This was one of those times.

That morning we'd had great sex, not like we'd had in months. It felt so right to be with her, the special intimacy of knowing each other for years.

Finally, we pried ourselves apart, showered and had coffee. The trip to the airport was pleasant, her hand in mine like it should be. We seemed to be getting along better than we had in months. She checked her baggage to the guy out front of the airport and just before she headed in to get her ticket and board, she turned to me.

"I'm sorry for being a brat, Cliff. I love you and can't wait to be able to take care of you as you have taken care of me for the last few years."

"I love you too, I'm sorry for being an asshole. I just want things to be back like they use to be."

When she gazed at me with her beautiful green eyes with hazel specks, I couldn't wait for her to get through with this week and return so we could try to repair the damage we had created. We kissed one last time and squeezed each other goodbye.

I thought I would surprise her, so I spent the next day thoroughly cleaning the house. I scrubbed the floors, vacuumed and dusted, and cleaned the bathroom until it sparkled only to have my cup of coffee slip out of my right hand the next day as I was standing at the little table where we kept the phone. The cup hit the table and coffee flew, spraying the walls, table and floor. It even sprayed a couple of pictures on the wall of Silly and me on our trip up the California and Oregon coast. Luckily it did not get behind the glass and ruin the photos. I took the pictures down and washed the sticky coffee off of the walls, table and pictures. I dried them and set them down on the table wanting the walls to dry before I re-hung them.

The next day I was anxious for Silly to return, missing her in our bed, missing spooning up to her and holding her tight, missing watching her stand at her dresser looking for clothes to wear. I liked to watch her beautiful tan body as she went through her clothes deciding what to wear for the day. She knew I loved her in little cotton summer dresses and sarongs, with cute little panties and open-toed shoes. No question, she was hot.

It was a gorgeous blue sky day, a great day to ride the new bike. One of my favorite rides was to Freeport and down to the river to Isleton. Silly and I loved this ride as it was scenic with many orchards, ranches and free of traffic. One of the usual stops on this ride is a little local bar in Freeport. As I walked in I noticed a table with four women all dressed in black. I took a seat at the bar, ordering a beer from the cute Latina bartender who had nice long dark hair, caramel skin, and a pearly smile.

As I sat there drinking my ice-cold beer, one of the ladies dressed in black asked if she could buy me a beer.

"No thanks," I said. "I just bought one. Thanks for the offer though."

As I was about to walk out the door, the woman said, "Oh come on, you have to have a beer with us, we just came from a funeral right next door."

I reluctantly stopped by their table. I really did not want to, yet at the same time I wanted to show some empathy. If I didn't work in the medical field, I probably wouldn't have stopped and sat down.

"Oh, I'm sorry to hear this." I replied. "I guess I can't turn you down, then."

As I pulled a chair out in between the tables, I noticed the lady had a cast on her left leg from the knee down. She was older maybe fifty and had blond Q-Tip fine hair. The wrinkles around her mouth and eyes and that leathery looking skin, told the story of years of smoking.

Her name was Sally. She introduced me to her friends and told me the funeral had been for a son of another friend who was killed in an accident.

I expressed my condolences.

"Nice bike," she said, peering out the window.

"Thanks, I actually just bought it."

"Have you heard of Slew House?" she asked.

"Is that the place out past Folsom by Sutter Creek that has the bands and barbecues for bikers?" I asked.

"Yeah. It's a great place if you like to ride and party."

"Heard about it but never been," I replied. "I was just telling some friends of mine from Reno about it. They are coming down this weekend on their bikes, and my girlfriend is coming back from San Diego this week. It would be cool to take them all out there."

"My husband and I live right across the street," she said. "Looks like you have two helmets. Let's go, I will show you where it's at."

"Are you sure? What about your cast?"

"Oh, no problem," she said. "I had a little surgery four weeks ago. They are supposed to remove this in a couple weeks. I'm fine."

"Are you sure?"

"No problem, I ride on the back of my husband's all the time. I'll leave my car here and you can bring me back."

"Sounds good, let's roll."

It was only four or five p.m. I figured we had plenty of time, even though I wasn't sure where it was.

As we headed out of town on Franklin, she tapped me on the shoulder.

"Hey, there's another little bar I'd like to show you!" she yelled.

I was never one to say no to a cocktail, yet I really didn't want to stop. We had just gotten going not ten minutes ago. I was a little uncomfortable with her on the back, her dragon breath on my neck. I wished it was Silly back there, her warm arms around my waist. But thought it would be rude to say no. She was doing me a favor showing me Slew House.

The bar was a dank shit hole smelling of old smoke. Sally knew the bartender, a little skinny man with his few strands of hair swept to the side. It was a local's place, full of drunks. I ordered a jack and coke draining it rather quickly, not wanting to stick around. The welcome warmth of the booze flooded through my veins.

I was able to hustle her back outside. At this point, I wanted to get this over with. A little guilt crept through me about having another woman on the back of the bike in Silly's helmet. I stuffed that feeling deep down inside me. *Let's just get there and back*, I thought, my eye on the prize.

The sun was hanging low in the sky. The day had about three hours of light left. I didn't have my nighttime glasses because the bike didn't have saddlebags. I had to get back before dark, I was hesitant.

Slew House was way out in the farmland of Folsom, nothing but green fields and cows. No city lights or street lights. I had no idea there was this much farmland out here. Once we arrived, she ordered another drink. You can't go into a bar and not have a drink, can you? That's how I was raised: you hit a bar, you have a drink. Or you're a pussy. Excited to know where Slew House was, I figured I could relax a little. Again, Sally knew the bartender, a woman in her thirties, dark hair and a pretty face. Once again I had a Jack Daniels and coke served in a 16-ounce glass, more Jack than coke. In two minutes I'd pounded it down. I hadn't eaten since breakfast so the drink lit me up. Immediately Sally handed me another. She might not have been attractive but she was efficient. And she was of my tribe: those who dig bikes and bars.

The room swayed a little. It was 8 p.m. I had until 9 p.m. to get back to town before it would be dark. And I had to open the department up at 5 a.m. *Shake it off*, I said to myself. *I can handle this. I've handled much more than this in my life.* We headed out.

Not more than ten minutes down the road, she once again tapped me on the shoulder.

"Hey, there's one other biker bar I want to show you," she said. When I turned to hear her better, her booze and cigarette dragon breath hit my face. She squeezed her arms around me tighter, while rubbing my chest. Silly. Where was my Silly? The one who loved to rub my pecs. I got an uneasy feeling. I just wanted to get home now, but at the same time, I did not want to come off as a pussy.

Once inside, déjà vu. She knew the bartender. We were served drinks: sixteen ounces of Jack, with a hint of coke. Seemed the barkeep just waved the coke bottle over the glass this time. Even though I was buzzed, I was missing Silly, grateful for her youth, vitality and beauty in comparison to this old whisker biscuit. What a lucky man I was to have her. Why was I sitting there with this old boot?

One, two, three more drinks. Shit, I'd lost track of the time. Glancing at the clock on the wall, I saw it was 11:30 p.m. We had to get the hell out of there.

As I was trying to pull the bike off the kickstand, it felt as though I was wrestling with a bull. My Old Uncle Pat, a biker, who used to ride an old Pan Head Chopper in the late '60s early '70s the kind with a twelve-foot-long front end, used to say, "If you can pull the bike off the kickstand you can ride it." I yanked the bike up. I could do this.

In my jeans, boots and a tank top, I rode through the dark of night, the dairy land of Folsom, moist and cold. Sally, heavy with drink, swayed all over the back seat as if she were unconscious.

It was difficult to see through my sunglasses; I could barely see three white lines ahead of me on the road. I pulled them off. Bugs and wind blurred my eyes. I was in serious trouble. I shoved the glasses back on. No better. God, I was chilled to the bone. I just wanted to get home and get some sleep.

The white lines flew past. On a straight stretch of road, I grabbed a fistful of throttle. The sooner I could flop down on my bed, the better.

The bike started to climb a small hill and head around a curve. Where the hell were we? I wanted to ask Sally, but she was out, barely hanging on, swaying from side to side.

Street lights. A curb. A traffic island.

Oh, holy hell. We were headed for an intersection going seventy miles per hour.

My mind flashed to a time in Reno on my old Full Luxury Hog. I had jumped a curb and island, missing the light pole. I was Superman. I could do this again. The last thing I remembered was hitting the curb and trying to pull the handlebars up.

As I started to wake up, I thought I was at home in bed. I was expecting to feel my soft pillows, blanket and Silly's warm, smooth body next to me.

But, wait, there was something cold, hard and wet against my face. Watery lights. Blue and red. Flashing.

I gagged. Someone was trying to shove something down my throat.

Where was I? What was happening?

A voice barked out something. Something that sounded like, "I don't think she's going to make it."

Oh my God. I killed Silly. Did I? Did I kill Silly?

My left leg. Something was wrong with my left leg. I felt down. It wasn't where it should be. As I turn my head to the left I saw the toe of my boot at neck height. My foot still in it. Reality pounced on me like a mountain lion. *I've done something horrible. Silly will leave me. She'll think I was on a date. I will lose my job. I am in Lovelock being sentenced again.*

Hands are reaching for me, lifting me. I'm being strapped to a stretcher, slid into the ambulance.

"Please," I say. "Please call Mercy San Juan Hospital and tell them I won't be in this morning to open the department."

Chapter 22: State of Mind

It must have been two or three in the morning when I woke up on an x-ray table at U.C. Davis.

As the x-ray tech was trying to position me on the table, I said, "I'm an x-ray and a nuclear medicine tech. Can you tell me how bad it is?"

He shook his head. "You do not want to know."

My gut wrenched. *Had I lost my leg?* I imagined myself, with no leg and no hands. Then I passed out.

Two days later my mind was still not clear. I was on so much morphine I had no idea what I damaged. When I tried to move from the waist down, it hurt like hell.

The doctor stood over my bed, unsmiling.

"You shattered your left femur in three complete pieces," he said. "You're very lucky that you look like you worked out a lot with weights. If you didn't have thirty-five inch thighs you would have lost your leg.

The fact that you had such strong upper leg muscles is the reason you still have your leg."

He then informed me I had shattered my left pubis ramous, which makes up a lot of the hip joint. He added that I tweaked my sacroiliac joints so bad in my pelvis I would be crooked and have a lot of pain in my future. I'd also broken ribs and my shoulder and maybe some closed-head trauma.

The severity of my pelvic and leg pain overrode all other sensations. I even hit myself in the ribs and shoulder and didn't feel a thing.

I soon learned from a nurse that Sally, my passenger, had broken her elbow, scapula and jaw. I felt horrible. It was one thing to hurt myself but another person? It was all my fault. Dear God. I had created another dramatic mess.

A million thoughts flooded my morphine-clouded head. Nine months ago when I graduated and was making plans with Silly had been the happiest time of my life. And I had just ruined it all.

Karma kicked my ass. I'd been acting like I was invincible drinking and riding like hooligan. Maybe I had gotten too cocky, too big headed and too big for my britches, too self-absorbed. I was only thinking about myself. How I had just gone through prison and continued straight with schooling for seven years. Figuring I owed myself this time of partying and recreation, yet not considering other people's feelings, mainly Silly's. Karma slammed my head into the pavement at 70 MPH.

The police report stated that kids at a Dairy Queen heard a loud crash at midnight and saw sparks, metal and bodies flying. It took the ambulance forty-five minutes to arrive. I was found eighty-six feet from the bike. We were fortunate no one ran over our motionless bodies.

I wondered what it must have looked like to a bystander. Maybe like Evil Knievel's crash at Las Vegas, when he ended up 100 feet from the bike. He flew through the air then rolled on the pavement like a lifeless, limp, rag doll, his bones bending like taffy. Evil Knievel broke his femur, his pelvis, his ribs and clavicle along with his back, in that accident. Just like me, only I was lucky not to break my back.

The police report also charged me with a DUI. When I called my old friend Joe in Reno. I said, "I can't believe they are giving me a DUI. Not a DUI."

He laughed. "What did you expect?"

Exactly. Not thinking, I wasn't expecting anything. I was letting the booze and adrenaline do my thinking for me. And now, that just cost me my life.

And with bodily injury, it was a felony DUI. I was sunk. Just the word *felony* made my stomach clench. What would happen to me and to all that hard work I'd done to get my licenses? What would happen to Silly and me? What had I done to my life?

I was so out of it from all the morphine, I didn't even know what day it was, or how many days had gone by. I was constantly in and out of consciousness. Silly had called my work, only to be told by my supervisor that I'd been involved in a near-fatal accident and had been transported to UC Davis Trauma Center.

She promptly called my sister and the first thing she asked my sister was, "Did he have another woman on the back?"

"Yes," my sister said. "He did."

My first phone call from Silly at UC Davis Trauma Center went like this: "Is there a nurse there sucking your dick?"

I was so full of morphine and in pain, these words were like a toreador coming at a raging bull.

"Shut the fuck up!" I yelled.

"You fucking liar," she said. "Your sister told me there was a chick on the back of your bike."

"Silly, I had just met the bitch at Freeport bar. I did not even want to talk to her, but she told me she and her husband lived across the street from Slew House and wanted to show me how to get there. You have to believe me, she was only showing me where Slew House was. I even told her I wanted to take you, Chance, Jessie, Robert and Peggy there this weekend."

"Liar." The phone went dead.

My parents came up from Reno to stay at our home. When they came to see me, they said I looked like I had been hit by a bus. I assured them I felt like it too.

"Silly is very hurt, Cliff," my mom said.

"I didn't even know that woman," I said, feeling more desperate than angry by this point. "She was only showing me where Slew House was. I even told her about Silly and the fact I wanted to take her and my friends there this weekend. It sure in the hell was not a date."

"She just doesn't understand, Cliff. She's thinking about moving out. We asked her not to. We said if she's mad she should just move into the spare room and treat you like shit for a couple months, but don't leave him now. Not after you've just taken care of her for the last couple years."

Over the next days, my parents and I begged Silly not to leave me like this. Nonetheless she was busy packing her bags.

When she finally meandered into the hospital to see me, I was busy trying to sit up, and in so much pain I was crying. She stopped at the door for moment and watched me. As she slowly walked in in a new mini skirt, she looked beautiful. Her hair looked lightened and her skin extra tan from the sun in San Diego. Her body was flawless, as beautiful as the day I had met her. Her body was perfect. Mine was broken. And my heart was, too. I knew she came by to tell me good-bye.

Hovering over me, she had a blank look in her emotionless eyes. She touched the side of the gurney, but not me.

I was crying.

"Silly, please you have to listen to and believe me. There was nothing going on, I didn't know her."

"It doesn't matter, Cliff. I am moving out." Conviction rung out in her voice.

"Please don't leave me like this," I begged.

She told me she'd been hired by USGS and her office was on the California State University campus in Sacramento.

"My new boss needs someone to house sit for him. I volunteered. It's for three to four weeks. This will give me time away, time to think."

"No, please don't leave me like this, Silly."

"I have to go now. Take care, Cliff."

"God, no, don't leave me like this." I was crying in front of her in a way I never had before. "If I broke your heart, you have to let me be the one to repair it. Please."

She walked out the door and out of my life, as simple as that.

Four weeks later when I was released from the hospital, my neighbor Matt came to pick me up in my truck. It would be big enough to get my leg in, which was stiff from a femoral rodding.

There was no way I could squat down into a car. Just trying to slide onto the seat of my truck struck me with excruciating pain.

My niece had to come from Reno to help me out. I couldn't stand very long or even walk more than a couple steps. The pelvis is the center of gravity. When you move any part of your body, it affects the pelvis. Now that I was off the morphine drip, every movement hurt. Furthermore, the room would start to spin, and I would get very dizzy whenever I went from laying down to sitting up or vice versa. Whenever I hit that forty-five-degree angle I'd almost pass out. I decided not tell the doctor about this. I didn't need my work or driver's license revoked.

It was all I could do to walk a block down the street and back. Knowing I needed compassion and incentive, my friend Joe came up from Reno. He would make me get up and walk up and down the street.

"Damn it, Cliff," he'd yell. "You can do this. You've been through worse and always had the guts to overcome. You have to dig deep now. You can't give up."

I wasn't sure I could bounce back from this one like I had all the rest. The pain was wearing me out. I felt like I had aged eighty years. I was always tired and hurting. The only thing that relieved the heartache and depression was to sit in the sun on the back porch and read my Bible. But the minute I turned away from those pages I felt like God turned his back on me. Or had I turned my back on God? I continually cried my eyes out. I had just destroyed my future.

I thought if only I could get my hands on a gun, I could be free from this grief. Or maybe I should hang myself. Or maybe overdose. But I was sure that suicide would be a one-way ticket to hell. I needed to deal with the shitty hand that God dealt me.

Eventually, though, even the threat of hell didn't stop the fantasy of being free of this earthly pain.

One evening I wrapped a power cord around my neck and tied it to the rafter in the ceiling. I leaned over, feeling the tug of the cord against my throat. Testing it. Just to see what it felt like.

Tears poured from my eyes.

I remembered a painting I had once seen of people with long spoons and forks as their arms and hands too long to feed themselves. In one section, the people were withered and sad because they were starving. In the other scene, the people were happy and enjoying themselves… because they were feeding each other. The miserable people were in hell. They were too focused on feeding themselves. The happy people were in heaven. They fed each other.

Deep down I knew I could find heaven somehow by getting out of the hell of my own pity party. I needed to find some heart, to stick

"What do you mean?" she asked.

"One of the female radiologists told me you called her and left a message that I was yours and she had better keep her distance."

"Well, who are the females in your phone?"

"Silly, I have many females in my phone, bankers, nurses, doctors." I said. "This is unacceptable; why would you do this? If I didn't love you. I would not be with you."

"Maybe you don't love me." She looked down at her plate of food then back in my eyes. "I don't think you know how much I love you."

I was fuming. This felt like blackmail. I did love her, but I wasn't going to say it right then just to placate her.

I was suffering from a hangover and not in a good mood. My head was pounding like a jackhammer going through concrete. My stomach felt like I had the flu. It was Thanksgiving and we were headed over Donner Summit to my parents' house in Washoe Valley for the holiday. My hangover exacerbated my bad mood, and I felt myself go on the attack.

"Silly, why did you call the doctor and tell her to stay away from me? Along with the other people in my phone?"

"I don't want you talking to other women. I told you that." She looked out her window at the dark pines flying by.

"I'm not twenty-four years old I have an important position in the medical field. I have large banking transactions. It's normal for me to have the numbers of women who are doctors, nurses, bankers and people at the radiopharmecies."

Knowing how irate I was, she said nothing. She just folded her arms and stared out the windshield. A horrible feeling grew in me. An irrational feeling. A feeling that I wanted to say something to hurt her.

"I don't think I even love you anymore." As soon as it was said, I knew I shouldn't have, but the mean words kept flying out of my mouth.

"I'm not even attracted to you anymore." I said. "Your actions have made you ugly to me. I want the ring back. Maybe we should take it one day at a time."

She started to cry. The more she cried, the more horrible I felt. I wanted to apologize but my tongue felt stuck. I wanted to reach and grab her hand like I usually did as we drove, or walked or even strolled the grocery store. Yet something kept me from doing it.

I didn't mean what I had said. I'd just wanted to lash out at her. I gripped the steering wheel, my head throbbing.

The rest of the way to my parents was silent. I felt my heart breaking, but it was if I wore Hannibal Lector's mask and could not speak.

When we noticed the home next door was vacant, I approached the owners and made a rent-to-own arrangement. I repainted the entire place wanting, a fresh start. It seemed as though Silly and I were starting to get back into the groove. She had created a little garden area in the yard. Blackberry vines crawled over the fence out back, and Silly made turnovers with the delicious fruit. After getting up at 4:30 a.m. to go to the gym together, I'd cook us breakfast while she packed our lunches before we left for work. It seemed maybe we were getting over our issues.

Soon after moving into our new house, I went to a motorcycle shop down the street from my work where I'd heard there were good deals on some nice bikes. For the last three years, I'd been riding my Harley FLH. It was a beautiful custom bike, with the fairing, hard bags, stereo, windshield and custom pearl paint with billet wheels and rev tech brakes. The brakes were so touchy that any mechanic that rode it would almost end it. However, I needed that style brakes to stop the bike with my right hand since I didn't have a great grip. I would always joke that FLH meant Full Luxury Hog. It is the most comfortable style bike they make. Yet, all my friends were riding Dyna Wide Glides and Fat Boys around and handle the challenges of my life.

When I could get around and about a little more I spent my days in the little Baptist church down the street. I didn't care what denomination it was. All I knew is when I walked in, I felt something deep, something that tensed my throat and caused tears to pour down my face. The crying felt good, it felt right. Like it was cleansing me, bringing me to someplace I needed to be. A relief.

I met the pastor, a good-sized man with graying hair. He had a very kind demeanor. He helped me write a letter to Silly's mother. I apologized for everything I'd done and told her I couldn't picture my life without Silly.

Every other day I sent a dozen roses to Silly's work. I'd call and plead with her to see me and listen to me. She just kept saying the same thing over and over. "I am never coming back."

For his services and help, comfort, sympathy and empathy, I gave the Pastor a drawing I'd done in prison of Jesus Christ. It was one of my finest pieces, done in pointillism. It had taken me over 300 hours to complete. I'd been waiting to buy a house with Silly to have it framed to hang on our wall.

I was now thirty-five years old. My body not healing like it used to. But I was determined to get back in shape. I couldn't sit around and mope about Silly any longer. I was trying to strengthen my core by doing many sit ups and abdominal exercises. I did push-ups and tried to get stretched back out. The first week I started going on walks, I made it a mile. Three months after the accident, I was able to run three miles a day. By then, I was back at work, even though I'd been told I'd be out six to nine months. For months I pulled call twenty-one days straight, took two days off and did it again. Work distracted me from the mess of my life.

When I felt ready to start dating again, I met a woman on line.

Zalina. She was very beautiful, built like a brick shit house with gorgeous curves. African American, she had beautiful hazel eyes and a beautiful smile to match her dazzling personality. After meeting for coffee a few times, we spent the day together at the zoo. After lunch, we came back to my place. We were sitting next to each other on the couch talking and joking around. It felt good to laugh. It had been a long time. She placed her hand on my leg and leaned over and kissed me.

"That was nice," I said.

"You're a great kisser," she replied, placing her hand on my chest. "Wow, you're solid."

"I try to stay in shape. It's been a few months since I've been to the gym though."

"Well, you look and feel good to me, Are you hard all over?" she asked while lowering her hand from my chest to my crotch.

"I'm sure I soon will be, if not already."

We continued to make out, kissing each other with great passion. It had been a while since I'd felt such an attraction for someone other than Silly. This was new and exciting.

But Silly's words echoed in my mind, *I'm never coming back.*

I pushed those thoughts aside, caught up in lust for Zalina. I craved being wanted. It was not that I wanted to make love to her, like I did Silly. I just wanted to have sex. I wanted the excitement and the passion. When we slid down onto the couch, she let me lie between her legs. Beneath her skirt, a tiny Mohawk of dark curly hair poked out the top of her low-cut pink panties. A shudder of excitement ran through me I started to kiss her, working my way to her firm and protruding nipples. She pushed at my shoulders, forcing me down to her privates. I could smell her and taste her. I had to have her now!

"Look, babe there's something I have to tell you."

"What is it?"

"About a year ago, at work I poked myself with an HIV

contaminated needle. I had to take some very potent drugs to kill the virus. I've been checked three times and have not contracted the virus; there's a very good chance I never will. However, it would be best if we use a condom."

"Do you have one?" she asked.

"Come with me," I said, leading her by the hand to the bedroom. I had condoms in the nightstand.

Out the window sat Silly's silver Subaru. A wave of fear ran through me. I hurried Zalina into the bedroom and shut the door, telling her I was going to put some music on. Had Silly's sister Anette seen me pull up with Zalina? Was Silly here to start some drama? Sure enough, I saw Silly walk towards the front door. Here she came in her little yellow flower print summer dress that she knew I loved, sporting her open toed sandals. Her hair glistening in the sunlight. I rushed to lock the door before I turned on the music.

Of course, she would show up now. I'd been sitting here wanting and waiting for her, alone for three or four months.

Silly knocked. I didn't answer, standing aside the door hoping she couldn't see me through the curtains. Then I slipped over to the back door and locked it. Maybe she'd think I wasn't home.

Why was she here now? Why could she not have called me and let me know she was thinking of me? Oh, God, why was Zalina here? This was my chance to finally be with Silly.

"Cliff, are you coming?" Zalina called out. "Hurry I've soaked through my panties."

"I'll be right there, babe," I said as quietly as I could.

Back in the bedroom, I lay on the bed next to Zalina. We started to make out again.

After about ten minutes, I figured Silly probably left. What a relief. Maybe she'd come back another time, and I'd be alone.

I reached for the condoms Silly had brought home from her

gynecologist. Here I was using Silly's condoms on another girl.

We got naked and Zalina put the condom on me. As difficult as it was, I started to make love to her. Trying to put Silly out of my mind.

The next thing I knew Silly was standing outside our bedroom window. I don't think she saw us, rather heard us.

"Hey you slut in there! Did he tell you he poked himself with an HIV contaminated needle?"

"What the? Who the? What's going on?" Zalina asked with a startled look on her face, rolling out from under me.

"Who the hell is that?" she whispered.

"Oh shit, my ex."

"Oh great," Zalina replied. "I thought you said she moved out months ago."

"She did. I have no idea why she's here."

"Let me in!" Silly screeched.

"You two still have ties?" Zalina asked.

"No babe, I don't know why she's here."

"Well sounds like you better let her in," she said. "Maybe I should leave?"

"No, you don't have to."

"Well, let her in and see what she wants."

I got up and put on my shorts.

When I opened the door, Silly came barging in.

"Who is this woman in my house?" Silly demanded.

"Your house? You moved out, remember?"

"Who is she?"

"Hello, I'm Zalina." Zalina, now dressed, walked into the room. "We just met recently. Cliff told me you two broke up."

"Get out of my house!" Silly ordered.

"No," I said. "She doesn't have to leave." I said. What a miserable moment. Here I'd wanted Silly to come by and surprise me with a visit like this for three months. I had been here alone pining away, waiting for her to come back. Finally, I try to move on, and now this.

"No Cliff, that's alright. It looks like you two aren't finished yet."

"Silly you told me you were never coming back. Remember, you left me."

"I came over today to tell you that I wanted to come back. And look at what you're doing!"

"You were never coming back!"

Silly headed for the door. I must have looked like a lost puppy. Tears started to flow from my eyes.

"Go ahead Cliff, go get her back if you want to," Zalina said.

"Are you sure?"

"Looks like you two are still in love to me."

"Thank you for understanding," I said.

I ran out the front door, chasing the Suburu which was headed down the street, calling her name. I ran past the neighbors' houses hoping no one was watching. It was hot out and my bare feet were burning on the pavement, but I didn't care.

The brake lights lit up. She had pulled over at the street corner. I was hoping she would wait for me.

"Stop, just stop so we can work this out!" I yelled at her.

When I reached her, she was sitting in the car crying.

"You told me you were never coming back!" I was panting out of breath. "What was I supposed to do? You left me four months ago."

"I thought I would come back to you today." Tears streaked her face. My heart, which had been healing, was breaking all over again.

"Please, come back. I've missed you and want you back!"

"How can I after this?" she said, clenching the steering wheel.

"You told me repeatedly you were not coming back. What was I supposed to do? Stay alone all my life?"

"I even shaved my unit for you!" she screamed. "I am leaving you now, and I'm never coming back." She shoved her foot on the gas and tore off.

It was like my wounds were ripped open. All the pain came flooding through me again. I just stood there, barefoot. Raw. Weeping in the street.

Needless to say, that was the last date for Zalina and me.

A while later, I met a woman named Helen who worked for the local news channel. Because the DMV canceled my license for the DUI, even though I had not been to court yet, Helen drove me to work and back. Sometimes she'd take time off her own job to help me out. Soon she took me to my court hearings as well, staying by my side the whole time.

I was very grateful to her. I don't know if I could have done it on my own. I felt like half the man I was before the accident. It seemed to rob me of at least half my energy, half my mobility and half my happiness.

Helen's roommate was the weather girl for a local news station. We all hung out, and I enjoyed cooking for them. These two beauties sat in my living room drinking wine and chatting, while I slipped into the kitchen to make us pizza.

And there in the kitchen, chopping tomatoes and grating cheese, I thought about how Silly and I use to do this together. Tears poured out. I had to dry them before going back into the living room.

One day a vase of flowers and a card appeared on my porch. They were from Sally, the passenger on the bike the night I wrecked. I was very surprised. I had no idea how she found out where I lived. In the card she said to give her a call, she wanted to know how court was going for me. She had written a letter to the judge. It stated that she had been the one to purchase all the drinks that night. She did not want me to be held responsible for her actions and her injures. She left her number in the card.

I called her and explained that my girlfriend had left me. I asked her if she could please call Silly or send her a letter explaining we were not on a date. She said she would but years later I found out she never did.

Donny Race, my new attorney, was a short plump, graying man, very polite and jovial. He told me he needed evidence of every stitch of education I'd received from prison on. He wanted to show how hard I had worked to get from being an inmate to being a productive member of society.

Every time I went to court, my blood pressure would rise. I'd get nervous, my palms sweaty. After dealing with Lovelock, I couldn't stand the idea of being in court. For years now I'd repressed that fear, and here I was, digressing.

"I see that this guy has done time," said the judge sternly as he peered through his wire rim glasses at Donny. "And I can also see what he did to better himself. I have never seen someone do what this guy has done. I believe he is a good guy deep down. If I give him a felony, will he lose his licenses to work?"

"Most likely, Your Honor," said Donny.

"Okay," said the judge, fixing me with a stare. "I'm going to charge you only with reckless driving. But you are getting a felony sentence: ninety days' house arrest. DUI classes along with Alcoholics Anonymous five times a week, and probation for a year."

I swallowed hard, trying to get the lump in my throat to go down. Shit, I did not want probation, but it was better than the alternative.

"Thank you, your honor." I replied. I shook Donny's hand and thanked him also for doing such a good job.

When I checked into the sheriff's office, I was fitted with an ankle bracelet and a Breathalyzer. I had to always be no more than eighty feet from the remote in the house or it would go off. Whenever I heard a loud beep from the Breathalyzer I had sixty seconds to get to it and breathe into it. Sometimes it would buzz at midnight. I almost didn't make it a few times. I also had to report to the sheriff's office once a week for a urine test. Here I go again, back under the thumb of the law. I thought I would never be under these circumstances again. How humiliating, how inconvenient.

I didn't mind not drinking. I did not miss it. My friends never tempted me. In fact many of them slowed down themselves after this happened. I did not miss the hang overs and the weight gain. Because I didn't receive a DUI, I was able to get my driver's license back as soon as I proved to the DMV I had only received a reckless. I had to attend many A.A. meetings along with a state run DUI class once a week. I hated the A.A. meetings, the same people telling the same stories. It was hard to try to stay awake through these monotonous tales. However, I did enjoy the state DUI classes. I re-learned a few things that we had gone over in some psychology classes. Addictive/dependent personality. I had to re-learn most of my drinking and partying was more of a habit, than a disorder. And I had the power to control it.

Then I received a letter in the mail. It stated that the woman on the back of the bike, whom I had not heard from in while now, was suing me for seven hundred and fifty thousand dollars. She thought I was a doctor. I was glad to receive her letter to the judge before this had happened. In fact my insurance attorneys used her letter against her. She ended up with fifty thousand; the coverage I had on the bike took care of it.

One day after I'd been back to work for about six months, two sheriffs, a slim man and a fat woman, walked in and were talking to my supervisor. I had sheriff phobia and got a flash of nervousness. My supervisor called me over and led the cops and me into a room on the side of the department.

"I don't know how a person like you gets a job like this," said the woman sheriff.

"Probably, unlike yourself, I have an education." I knew being snitty wasn't the best idea, but I couldn't help myself. *Who did she think I was?*

"How did you get to work today? You have no license!"

I looked at her and laughed.

"I drove my car."

"You broke the law. We're taking you in now. Your license was revoked for a DUI."

"No, I didn't break the law. I have a driver's license."

"How could that be?" she asked, glaring at me with her fat, double chinned jaw wide open.

I pulled my newly reinstated license out and showed it to her and the other officer.

"We'll just see about that," she puffed, in disbelief.

Her colleague called DMV to check it out. I was in tears laughing now as I heard the DMV tell him, "He was not charged with a DUI, he was charged with a reckless and yes his license is valid."

In disgust they both put their tail between their legs and she waddled out. Never to be heard from again.

Every time I heard a Harley go down the street, I would start to sweat and get short of breath. All the pain, both mentally and physically, had now taken its toll on me. The physical pain and the loss of Silly hurt more than the incident at Lovelock. In fact, the heartache was more intense than the physical trauma. Combined, they would soon drain me of my youth and patience. I was always tired and in bed by 8 p.m. If I stayed up late, I felt hung over the next day. I felt as though I had been hit by a bus. I was running three miles a day, but every joint in my body hurt.

It took me almost a year to get all the legal responsibilities taken care of. When I had less than thirty days left on probation and house arrest, I slipped out during my lunch break to the same bike shop where I had bought my bike about a year ago.

"You're alive." The man who'd sold me the bike was still there. He had a smile on his face.

"Barely," I told him.

"We heard about the accident, and saw the bike. You are either one lucky or one tough son of a bitch to survive that."

"I'm not sure I did."

"What can I do you for?"

I was sick of the pain, sick of the fear. Something was keeping me awake at night. I knew as long as I let this fear beat me, I'd never be happy.

"I need a bike," I said. "I want another Springer."

"We don't have any Bad Boys, but I did just get this in two days ago."

He led me across the room. There sat a black and white 02 Springer with 1959 fenders and nostalgic look. Years ago in Big Ed's office there hung an old picture of James Dean; he sat on a bike that looked just like this. I had to have it.

"Do you mind if I take it for a spin?" I asked.

"No problem."

As I sat on the seat and started engine, the vibration and roar were soothing. Yet I was afraid to put it in gear. I sat there for a few moments.

"When you get bucked off, you get back on," I whispered to myself.

When I put it in gear and gave it gas, it responded nicely. My chest felt tight. Nervously, my palms damp, my ears ringing, I eased onto the street. When I hit the highway ramp, something clicked in my brain. It was like the shot of adrenaline I had needed, wanting, waiting for, like a junkie getting his fix. I grabbed a fist full of throttle.

Bam! The bike took off like a racehorse out of the starting gate. It almost slipped out from underneath me. I tightened my legs and ass, and hung on. My eyes on the road, I shifted lanes.

By the time I could looked down, I was doing 105 miles per hour and had plenty of throttle. I twisted the throttle all the way, leaving the traffic behind like it was standing still. I kept it nailed for a mile or two. Something inside me would not let go. All the fear evaporated. The needle throbbing over 130MPH, the cold rush of air, the G-force of the bike, and the sun golden hills flying by like my memories.

I headed back to the shop and bought the bike. The only stipulation was that they could not deliver it until I was off probation in four weeks. No one could see this bike at my home.

The day I got off the house arrest the bike was sitting in my garage.

I was ready to leave Sacramento. For two months I worked to line up a job in Reno at a local diagnostic center running their nuclear medicine department, and I bought a house there, too. On my last day of my probation and work, I happily pulled my house arrest equipment out of the saddlebags of my bike and returned it to the local sheriff's office. Then I popped in the hospital to gather my check. My saddlebags were packed for a 21-day trip through the Sierras. I needed a break; I needed the wind in my face once again.

I still had the head spins when I reached the 45-degree mark getting up or lying down. Sometimes I would almost pass out because of it. Now I was getting dizzy sometimes just standing still. One day I had to grab the wall and almost passed out at work in the hospital. I only hoped the vertigo would not hit me on the bike.

Then again, maybe it would be a good way to go. I could just pass out and crash, feeling nothing. I was mad at God for letting me live through this one. I hurt so much now both physically and mentally, I wished I hadn't made it through it.

Wearing shorts and sandals, I raced my new Harley through the Sierras, pine trees whizzing by. My anger built. At myself. At God. My vision smeared with tears. I hit the corners so fast I thought surely I wouldn't make it.

Grabbing a fistful of throttle, I yelled, "God! Come and get me now. Please!"

Chapter 23: Uncle Dan

Death by motorcycle was not meant to be. Once back in Reno, I started my new job, which was at an outpatient facility rather than a hospital. This environment was much easier on both the technician and the patients. We called the patients "Walkie Talkies" meaning they were walking and talking, unlike those in hospitals who are brought in on wheelchairs or gurneys.

I settled into this new life. I was making good money, I owned a nice home and I had time to get to the gym on a regular basis. I owned some of my favorite toys; a four wheel drive, my bike and some new fishing gear and tackle. During my time off I would cruise the Sierras on my bike, breathing in the smell of the pines and clean air looking for spots to drop the fishing line in.

Yet an ache nagged me, a feeling that something was missing. What was wrong? I didn't know. Something elusive. Perhaps I had too much money and time on my hands or wasn't challenged enough at work. And in spite of it all, I missed Silly Pepper.

My good friend Shane had a job as a traveling nuclear medicine tech. In order to lure me to join him, he started sending me photocopies of his paychecks: he was making about twelve thousand dollars a month. Soon I headed to the Human Resource department to give my two-week notice.

My first job was in Maine in January. It was easily 40 degrees below zero. I spent my time between work, gym and home: an old Victorian bed and breakfast. It was very comfortable and even had a fireplace. But as comfortable as it was, the weather wreaked havoc with my joints because of all my injuries. After getting home from the gym while lying in bed I could feel the breaks in my femur throbbing. If I got a call to go in at 1 a.m. I had the pleasure of shoveling three feet of snow to get to the car. Then of course there was the challenge of driving on ice. The hospital was small but unfortunately to get to it we had to park about a mile away. By the time I walked ten minutes in forty degrees below zero, I was wide awake and frozen.

My next job took me to Placerville, California just two hours from my home and on Highway 49. Famous Highway 49 runs through the Gold Rush mining towns. It was a direct route from Placerville to where I had my home in Sparks. Bikers appreciate this ride. The roadside is dotted with many green pastures and wildflowers in the Springtime. You pass a multitude of rivers, lakes and streams; you ride through mountains filled with pinion pines, and redwoods, and catch a glimpse of Daffodil Hill, which is a stunner when caught in the right season.

While working my travel assignment for nuclear medicine in Placerville, I stayed at a bed and breakfast, which also served as a wedding facility. My temporary home was the Gardner's Cottage a single-wide trailer decorated to make it looked like a quaint little cottage. It had a place to put the Harley, my main concern.

After a week or two I decided to visit with my aunt who'd lived in Placerville for the past twenty years. I hadn't seen Katy in a long time. But she was always fun to be around, that I could remember. We decided to meet at Sly Park Reservoir, where she and her boyfriend would be picnicking. I looked forward to the ride on the Harley through the beautiful pines and oaks, a bright green world over flowing with foliage.

At Sly Park, while eating under the trees, Katy asked me where I was staying. When I described the cute little trailer at Sun Rise's bed and breakfast, she looked at me in disbelief.

That was where, she said her ex-husband Danny was living eight years ago when an accident took his life while he'd been working for the owners of Sun Rise. The water truck he'd been driving had rolled down a hill. Pinned under it, he died.

I remembered Danny was a very large man, with long flowing brown hair down to his waist. He was always happy and laughing. It seemed they were always enjoying themselves. But I was only ten years old. What did I know?

When I returned from the picnic, I saw the Davises, the owners of Sun Rise, standing out front of the facility. I pulled up on my bike and informed them we had a mutual friend. As I talked about how Danny was actually related to me through my aunt, they were clearly amazed at the coincidence.

I was enjoying working at Marshal hospital but enjoying my time off even more taking great Harley rides around California's old mining country. In spring, the grass was vibrant green and smelled so sweet. Winding through the foothills and mountains all the way to Yosemite was magical. Pulling call on the weekends with my pager in my pocket could mean appearing in the ER wearing Harley boots, shorts and tank top beneath my lab coat. The female staff and some of the patients couldn't help but comment good-naturedly.

One evening while watching TV in the trailer, I saw something move out of the corner of my eye. I turned. Nothing. A few minutes later it happened again. The little hairs on my back and arms stood straight up. Something was very strange. Night after night this sense that I was not alone struck me.

One night while lying in bed, I was sure someone was right out my bedroom door making a metallic noise, like dropping coins or chains on the top of the metal washing machine. And it looked like shadows were moving in the living room and kitchen. I got up to look. Nothing.

Night after night it was the same thing: noise, movement. Nothing. Every time my body reacted like an electric current was running through my veins. I would put my earplugs in and keep my eyes closed tight, fearing what I might see if I opened them.

One Friday night, Mary came to visit from Sacramento. A probation officer for Sacramento county, Mary a gorgeous African American woman, stood six-foot tall and wore size five jeans. I enjoyed her company, admiring how well read she was. She had an incredible vocabulary. That night as usual, I grilled her a Boca Burger, teasing her about her vegetarian burgers being grilled, while grilling myself a steak.

I went to bed before Mary because I had to be up at 5:30 a.m. The next thing I knew Mary was shaking me violently.

"Wake up, wake up," she whispered. "There's someone in the house." I could tell by her voice she was scared. I figured she must have seen what I by now was calling *the ghost. The ghost of Uncle Dan.*

"Don't worry about it," I said, not even opening my eyes. I was really tired. I rolled over and fell back asleep.

Again, she shook me.

"There's someone walking around the house," she whispered furiously.

"Don't worry," I said. "It's just my Uncle Dan."

When I came home from work the next day, Mary clearly shook up said as we'd been lying in bed last night she watched a big man walk down the hall from the kitchen to our doorway. He'd stood there looking at us for about thirty seconds.

"He was very big and had long flowing hair down past the middle of his back," she said, her voice filled with disbelief. He then walked over to the bed, bent over and looked down at us. I was terrified. I thought he might kill us. But then he straightened up, walked back down the hallway and disappeared.

It was then I told her about the story of Uncle Dan and the unfortunate accident. She never did come and spend the night there again.

Mary confirmed for me what was going on in the trailer as I slept. For some reason, I could tell when he was around. The hair on my neck and back would let me know. I did not fear him, though. In fact, I felt as if he was family. I felt as if he was there for me. I do wish I had tried to speak to him now.

The next weekend was a big event in Placerville and all the rooms in the bed and breakfast had been previously booked in advance. I had agreed to move out of the trailer for that weekend. I went to Reno for the weekend, and when I returned I said to Carolyn Davis, "You know this place is haunted, right?"

"How do you know?" she asked with a peculiar look in her eyes.

After I told her about all my sightings and Mary's experience, she said, "The people who booked the trailer for the weekend had noticed someone was making noises at night, and that someone had taken the soap and shampoo bottles and lined them down the center of the tub!" She added that Uncle Dan was also hiding their robes and towels. Eventually the customers ran out of the trailer, screaming, swearing they would not spend one more minute in there.

The owners of the ranch purchased a house up on the hill from Sun Rise and asked me to stay there instead. The house had belonged to the now-dead grandfather of one of their employees. What a nice change from a haunted trailer to a big house. However, the same things started to happen in the house: I saw movements and vague objects from the corners of my eyes. Again, my hair stood on end. Did the grandfather haunt this place? Once again, I put in earplugs and clamped my eyes shut in order to sleep.

The next week or so, we got a new guy in the department to fill in for vacation and to help pull call. His name was Blain. He was very quiet and subdued I noticed. As we were talking, come to find out he also had a Harley and lived in Auburn, a town about an hour away through beautiful terrain. One day he mentioned his wife was a witch.

"You shouldn't talk about her that way," I joshed.

"No, really, she's a witch. She performs ceremonies, does psychic readings, and expels ghosts."

That's when I told him about what I had experienced at Sun Rise. I asked him, if he and his wife could come over and check it out. He thought that sounded like fun.

When Blain and Terra arrived, Carolyn and I met them at the gate. Carolyn talked about other strange occurrences throughout the ranch, including an old chair that Carolyn had received from an old neighbors house when the neighbor passed away. They were good friends, when the neighbor passed, Carolyn brought an old lounge chair of the neighbors that she had admired for years. She put the chair in one of the cabins they rented out for the bed and breakfast. There had been an increase in paranormal activity and strange things were happening in this cabin too. Along with the kitchen facility and restaurant in the main house.

At the cabin, Tera said she could sense an old female presence in the cabin where the old chair had been placed. It was if the ghost had come with and liked to stay in the chair. In the main house, Tera could sense Carolyn's grandfather, who we figured was waiting for Carolyn's mother to pass. Her grandfather built the ranch and main house. Her grandfather and mother were very close and from what Tera and Carolyn said they had an unusually close relationship, Electral love even. Tera gathered he was waiting there at the ranch for his daughter to pass. Carolyn's mother was in her later seventies and living above the ranch at that time.

We walked through the hot August day; it was close to 100 degrees, toward the Gardner's Cottage. While we waited, Tera approached it first, stopping at the window of the spare room where I often saw movement.

"I feel his presence," she said.

The front door was stuck. We tried to jiggle and push at it, but it wouldn't give. So finally we went around to the back door to let ourselves in. Inside, the trailer was boiling hot, 120 degrees. Even though the thermostat was off, the heater was blasting. As we opened all the windows and doors for air, Tera walked around. We followed nervously, like we expected something to jump out at us.

"This is where I feel him most," said Tera in the spare room and then the kitchen, the two places I often thought I saw things.

Back at the main house we sat and had coffee and were discussing Tera's findings. Tera said Uncle Dan was trying to get my attention to tell me something was going to happen. An Opt Out. He was telling me not to do something between September tenth to the twenty-fourth, only a week away. I had a choice, she said. If I rode my Harley on those dates, I would die in an accident. God had spared my life so many times and now it was up to me to decide whether I wanted to stay or go.

I sat there, stunned. This was my message? After all those times I'd begged God to take me while I flew around the Sierras' on the Harley, and now it was my call? Stay here or go home to heaven?

Everyone begged me to hand my keys over to Carolyn. She wanted to keep them for a week before, throughout, and a week after the dates given just to be sure.

I reached into my pocket, turning them over in my fingers. I held the keys in my hand. Just like I held my life in my hands.

Slowly, I pulled them out of my pocket and placed them in Carolyn's outstretched palm.

Epilogue: A Blessed Life

After I decided to live, life continued to roll on.

I found a fixer-upper in Washoe Valley, Nevada, the small valley where I'd grown up. I knew a few of the neighbors, and I had friends there, some from as far back as kindergarten. My parents lived down the street. It felt like I was home.

My work life in nuclear medicine morphed—and took a surprising turn. I met a man named John who had a thriving business dealing in new and used nuclear imaging equipment. He was an expert in a technique called *cedar gating*, heart software that detects how the heart is pumping. Continuing my nomadic ways, I began working for him at a center in southern California, far away from my new home.

I stayed in Corona with Martin. On my days off, I often rode my bike with my uncle, who had a Harley. We'd head off on highway 101 to San Diego through a beautiful area called Fallbrook, over to the ocean and down to San Diego. Other times we'd head up to Mt. Palomar or to the little mountain town of Julian. In spring, we rode along the miles of orange groves, the air thick with the scent of orange blossoms. This always made me think of Silly. When I'd been at Loma Linda, she'd held onto me as we traversed this same route, drenched in this alluring fragrance.

Southern California had its finer points, but I didn't like the crowds and traffic. I wanted to be closer to northern California and my home. As I was searching for a job, my sister suggested my cousin Mickey do a tarot reading for me to tell me what my future held. I'd had no idea she did readings. Lucy told me she'd witnessed Mickey predict that either she or her friend Tammy was pregnant with a girl. This was a surprise because they were both young and did not have babies on their minds. Nine months later, Tammy did in fact gave birth to a baby girl. My sister also told me that she'd asked Mickey to do a distance reading on me years ago—and she had correctly predicted I'd be sentenced in Lovelock. So it seemed they knew I'd be doing time before I did.

In my reading, Mickey saw two jobs. Both involved traveling; the job that paid the least amount would be the better opportunity. But the one I would take would be the higher paying position.

As she'd predicted, two jobs crossed my path. The lower-paying one was intriguing, but I was chasing the money. Also, the job was in central California, which allowed me to live at home and still travel. The job involved doing PET Scans, Positron Emission Tomography, it is a modality we use that has become very popular for searching for and detecting cancer, on a mobile coach that I would work on at various imagining centers throughout the central valley.

At another reading, Mickey informed me that I would be meeting a very small black man wearing glasses. One day I heard a knock on the door of the coach. I opened the door, looked out and saw no one. Then I heard a *hello*. I looked down to see a very small black man. He must have been a few inches short of five feet tall. Rolly polly, he seemed cheerful and wore wire rim glasses.

"I'm Henry, your new partner," he said, sticking out his hand.

Mickey's psychic powers were not to be messed with!

Eventually, tired of constantly moving around, I left the mobile coach job to work for a cardiac office in Modesto. The money was good. There I befriended Mike, another tech, who introduced me to John, an old friend of his. John crop-dusted for most of the local farmers in the area. Also a Harley rider, John and I hit it off as though we were old friends. Sadly, not two months later, John was killed in a plane crash.

The next week, during another reading, Mickey asked me if my father or grandfather were planning a plane trip. I didn't think so and asked why. She said she saw a plane crash with death around an older light-complected man. It was then that I told her about John's plane crash and death.

Mickey is usually right on and I continue to periodically call on her for readings. But with any reading there is always good and bad. I am not so good handling the bad. I become too consumed with worry. Maybe it's better to not fiddle with the future and just embrace life's mysteries.

Not one to settle in a job, I decided to start my own traveling business. I would contact cardiologists who needed a tech and have them sign a one-year contract. I did this for the next few years, writing off 50,000 miles a year on my 1099. I basically lived in the Hilton, or rented another home where ever work was, spending weekends at home in Washoe Valley.

One day I started to think about how much I missed creating art. Recently I had pulled out some of my previous work. I had been painting with oils and acrylics since age twelve, and had upped my art game in prison. I enjoyed graphite drawings, portraits, pastels, silhouettes, acrylic and oil paints and pointillism. In the evenings after work on a travel assignment, I went and purchased an art table and supplies to have with me while out of town. I started to draw a big-horned sheep in graphite.

I thought I should try to build my portfolio. Deep down, for much of my life, I'd dreamed of becoming a professional artist. I was now forty-five. Was it too late? Some days I thought: *Maybe not. After all, I graduated Loma Linda at thirty-four.* Other days I thought: *I will be in nuclear medicine until I die.*

I began to think about how lucky the people were who would be sitting in their homes enjoying their families. Every once in a while I'd date, but truth be told, I didn't have much of a personal life. I was working hard making money, my motivation for a lot of these years. But I was beginning to burn out. So much so that I started to dread leaving home on Sunday nights. I ached to be like those people who were in their cozy, familiar surroundings. But I forced myself to head out in my Toyota FJ Cruiser for the four or five hour drive through the snow of the Sierras. If I didn't head out the night before I would leave at 3 a.m., so I could arrive in time put in an eight-to ten-hour day.

When I was working on my art, I was happy. Work, I dreaded. I started to resent being in the medical world, surrounded by the smells and sounds of sickness, of hospitals and clinics. Honestly, I had never liked that environment much; how ironic that I had spent so much time in medical facilities as a medical professional and a patient. I knew these feelings were telling me there was something better than this. For years I had been motivated by money. I had the satisfaction of knowing I had reached my goal. But it wasn't as gratifying as I'd imagined it would be. There is more to life than money. And now I just wasn't satisfied having my life be consumed with work.

An unease, an emptiness, haunted me. I wanted to discover what would fill it.

One day at a local home improvement store, as I was loading large pieces of sheet-rock onto a cart, I felt something tear in my left arm. An ultrasound revealed I had torn my bicep. Not only that, it needed to be operated on within seven to ten days or the muscle would shrink and not be reparable.

Post-surgery I could not straighten out my last two digits on my left hand. Because of this when I would reach for something, I would drop it. Now it felt like I had no hands. At work I was at risk of dropping important things—like radioactive syringes and or isotopes. The reality was I could not practice radiation safety any longer. My career was over. But what would I do for money? I had sunk every penny I had in my home and could not afford to lose it.

After applying for disability, I spoke on the phone with an SDI agent.

"Have I been accepted?" I asked, praying I had.

"Are you kidding?" he said. "With all the injuries you have sustained, not just your hands but your pelvis and femur, how could we deny you?"

He saw that I had been on disability twenty years before and then put myself through school and worked another fifteen years.

"No one does that," he said.

Thank goodness everything fell into place. Still, though, I had no idea how I was going to manage on a fraction of what I had been making. There were some months I had no hot water or TV. Sometimes I'd run out of food and coffee before the end of the month.

I turned my focus to artwork and building my portfolio. Something magical happened whenever I was making art: I'd relax and feel at peace.

Soon, my artwork started selling. The old saying *Do what you love and the money will follow* was turning out to be true for me. I want to spend the rest of my life creating art.

When painting, I get lost in time. I feel like I'm my true self. Recently I have learned photography. Online, I met a Brazilian artist who taught me how to use software for photo manipulation, and in return I taught her painting.

Guided by a course at a local art museum, I relearned airbrush using my left hand instead of my right. I forced myself to rely only on my left hand by tying my right hand to my side. Finishing the class, I started a series of work that consisted of seventy pieces. I sold forty pieces for $500 to $5,000 each.

Since then, my work has been featured in juried art shows and has been part of the Country Music Awards and the National Rodeo Finals. At the last NFR in Las Vegas, two law professors from New York bought my off-the-wall skulls for $2,000 each. When I confessed that I had just cut the prices in half since it was the last day of the show, they admonished me.

"Never do that," said one professor. "We would have been glad to pay double. Your art belongs in New York art galleries and museums."

Of course this made me feel fantastic. It was like someone was raving about my own child. But ultimately, it's not external validation or the money that brings me the true joy of making art. It's the feeling that I am doing what I was put here to do: create.

In spite of all the extreme ups and downs of my life—or perhaps, because of them—I am grateful to be who and where I am. The chaotic energy of mayhem has taught me a lot. And now I am pouring that energy into my art. I have even named my business "Mayhem Mediums." It's a beautiful thing to not be governed by mayhem and instead to govern it. Havoc is no longer my middle name. I love my home and the area I live in. I am the grateful caretaker of my acre of land at the base of the Sierra mountains a mere forty-five minutes from beautiful Lake Tahoe. It is quiet here. Peaceful. I am surrounded by family and lifelong friends. I am doing what I love. God has blessed me well. Every single thing that has happened to me has brought me to this place. Each experience has made me who I am.

Acknowledgment

I would like to thank Cynthia Walker for her inspiration and hard work in encouraging me to write this book. She provoked the writing of this book after years of procrastination. Cynthia is also the first person to be kind enough to ghost write my first and original draft. I thank her for all her hard work and efforts. I would like to also thank Cheryl Young, artist, for introducing me to my editor, writing coach and teacher Kate Evans. Kate turned out to be the saving grace of my book. Her vast knowledge and expertise is what has transformed this book from an average read to an exceptional story. I appreciate her hard work and patience. She edited the book with a teaching method that helped me learn what to do as a writer. Kate is a fantastic author of the award-winning memoir, "Call it Wonder: an odyssey of love, sex, spirit, and travel" and the novel "For the May Queen." I would also like to thank Jan McCutcheon for her hard work in cover design and editing along with being my publisher. She had to put up with my picky artist ways in creating the cover. I thank Jan for her patience and professionalism along with her outstanding creativity. I could not have pulled this off without the help from these four wonderful women. I would also like to express my thanks to my parents and siblings who have had to endure the shenanigans and events in this book. I am sure it was no picnic on the lawn for any of them.

A special thank you my family and friends for the feedback and advice they offered after reeding through the original rough drafts, Cindy Capurro, Mickey Williams, Patrick O'Brien, Paige Oeding, and Cynthia Walker. And to my sister Kat for performing the last line edit.

Michael Clifford Helm was born in 1964 in Reno. A former cowboy, athlete, hairdresser, prison inmate, and nuclear medicine tech, he has lived many lives. Now a professional artist and published author, he lives in Washoe Valley, Nevada. www.Mayhem-Mediums.artistwebsites.com

Made in the USA
Middletown, DE
26 May 2019